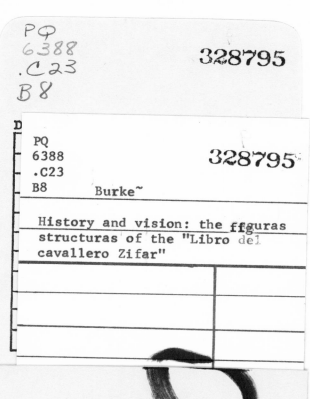

PQ
6388
.C23
B8   Burke~

History and vision: the ffguras
structuras of the "Libro del
cavallero Zifar"

328795

BRO
DART Printed in U.S.A.

HISTORY AND VISION:
THE FIGURAL STRUCTURE
OF THE «LIBRO DEL CAVALLERO ZIFAR»

JAMES F. BURKE

HISTORY AND VISION:
THE FIGURAL STRUCTURE
OF THE «LIBRO DEL CAVALLERO ZIFAR»

TAMESIS BOOKS LIMITED

LONDON

Colección Támesis

SERIE A - MONOGRAFIAS, XXVIII

Depósito Legal: M. 33.227 - 1972

Printed in Spain by Talleres Gráficos de EDICIONES CASTILLA, S. A.
Maestro Alonso 23, - Madrid

for

TAMESIS BOOKS LIMITED
LONDON

To Nancy, my wife

TABLE OF CONTENTS

PREFACE

Because the Libro del Cavallero Zifar *has received very little critical attention in the past, a number of basic problems remain to be solved. Some progress has been made in the study of the book's sources, its literary technique, and its relationship to other works of the period, though much research is still needed. Other aspects have been markedly neglected, and prominent among these is the possibility of a secondary or implied meaning in the* Zifar.

I became aware, while working on my doctoral thesis, that allegory (and I use the term in its broadest sense) was an important factor in the Zifar. *I did not deal with the problem at that stage, not only because it presents so many difficulties and complications, but also because I believed that other questions needed to be dealt with first. Since then I have become increasingly convinced of the central importance of the book's implied meanings. The present study is an attempt to discover what kind of interior significance exists in the* Zifar *and to explain how this secondary meaning functions as an essential complement to the actions of the knight and his family on the surface plane.*

A number of people have aided me in finishing this study. Views expressed by Dr. Roger Walker of Birkbeck College, University of London, when he visited Toronto in August, 1970, were helpful in deciding which route to follow in the final stages of preparing the typescript. Professor Martin Stevens of the State University of New York at Stony Brook kindly sent me a copy of an excellent paper on the liturgical drama which he had presented at the Western Michigan Conference on Medieval Studies in May, 1970. Professor J. H. Parker of the University of Toronto aided me in securing research funds. Professor G. L. Stagg also of the University of Toronto gave me encouragement, aided me in obtaining research funds, and suggested that I send the typescript to Tamesis for consideration. The University of Toronto Office of Research Administration provided funds which facilitated the gathering of material. The staff at both the University of Toronto Library and the Library of the Pontifical Institute of Medieval Studies were always most cordial in assisting me in my research. My students Miss Christine Isenman and Mr. Colbert Nepaulsingh read the typescript and made a number of valuable comments and suggestions. I am most grateful to Professor A. D. Deyermond of Westfield College, University of London, who read the typescript for Tamesis and whose comments and corrections were invaluable. He is of course in no way to be held responsible for the views which I present. This book has been published with the help of a grant from the Humanities Research Council of Canada using funds provided by the Canada Council. My gratitude to both agencies is very great.

In quoting medieval Spanish texts I have followed the edition utilized as closely as possible except that I have regularized u and v, i and j according to modern usage.

Toronto, Canada.   J. F. B.

ABBREVIATIONS

AHDE	*Anuario de Historia del Derecho Español.*
APSR	*American Political Science Review.*
BAE	*Biblioteca de Autores Españoles.*
BH	*Bulletin Hispanique*
BHS	*Bulletin of Hispanic Studies.*
CE	*Catholic Encyclopedia.*
CL	*Comparative Literature.*
CR	*Chaucer Review.*
CSIC	Consejo Superior de Investigaciones Científicas.
EL	*Estudios Lulianos.*
ELH	*Journal of English Literary History.*
HR	*Hispanic Review.*
HTR	*Harvard Theological Review.*
JEGP	*Journal of English and Germanic Philology.*
JHI	*Journal of the History of Ideas.*
JWCI	*Journal of the Warburg and Courtauld Institutes.*
KRQ	*Kentucky Romance Quarterly.*
LR	*Lettres Romanes.*
MLN	*Modern Language Notes.*
MLR	*Modern Language Review.*
MP	*Modern Philology.*
NBAE	*Nueva Biblioteca de Autores Españoles.*
NCE	*New Catholic Encyclopedia.*
NRFH	*Nueva Revista de Filología Hispánica.*
PL	*Patrologiae cursus completus... Series latina,* ed. J. P. Migne (Paris).
PG	*Patrologiae cursus completus... Series graeca,* ed. J. P Migne (Paris).
PMLA	*Publications of the Modern Language Association of America.*
QJS	*Quarterly Journal of Speech.*
RF	*Romanische Forschungen.*
RFE	*Revista de Filología Española.*
RH	*Revue Hispanique.*
RHF	*Revue d'Histoire Franciscaine.*
RP	*Review of Politics.*
RPh	*Romance Philology.*
RR	*Romanic Review.*
RTAM	*Recherches de Théologie Ancienne et Médiévale.*
SP	*Studies in Philology.*
Spec	*Speculum.*
Trad	*Traditio.*
UTQ	*University of Toronto Quarterly.*

INTRODUCTION

The anonymous *Libro del Cavallero Zifar* is the first of the Spanish romances of chivalry and was probably written shortly after *1301*. [1] Critics of Spanish literature have largely been willing to accept Ticknor's maxim that the *Zifar* and others of its genre might well «deserve the oblivion into which they have fallen». [2] The adventures expounded in these romances do not catch the interest of the modern reader. The morals are too obvious; there appears to be a lack of subtlety in the creation of character and event. It is likely, however, that these works were very popular among the literate of the late Middle Ages and the Renaissance. To characterize them as no more than «potboilers» is naive if we consider that the reading public was not large and that a romance of chivalry must have been composed for the same group that might have appreciated the *Libro de buen amor.*

The *Zifar* begins with a prologue in which the author relates how Ferrand Martines, the archdeacon of Madrid in the Cathedral of Toledo, brings the body of his former mentor Cardinal Gonzalo Gudiel to Toledo from Rome for burial. The trip was extremely arduous and the author of the romance (who may even have been Ferrand Martines himself) was impressed with the great loyalty and devotion which the archdeacon had shown toward his late patron.

After the prologue comes the first of three major divisions into which the work naturally divides —the «Cavallero de Dios y el rey de Mentón» section. The author of the *Zifar* connects the prologue to this division by implying that the «message» inherent in Ferrand Martines' deed is analogous in some way to what the hero Zifar will accomplish. The knight is descended from a family of kings which lost its former position of honor because of the evil deeds of one member. Zifar sets out with his family upon a quest which he hopes will restore the fallen family line. Once this restoration has been accomplished and Zifar has become a king, the tenor of the work changes and there follows a long segment in which Zifar and his two sons Garfín and Roboán are forced to defeat a traitorous vassal, the Count Nasón.

In sharp contrast to the action which fills the first major division, the «Castigos del rey de Mentón» section is completely static. Zifar through page after page advises his sons concerning the duties of a knight and the responsibilities of the king. This division very likely is based upon the *de regimine principum.*

[1] See Erasmo Buceta, «Algunas notas históricas al prólogo del *Cavallero Cifar*», *RFE,* XVII (1930), 18-36.
[2] George Ticknor, *History of Spanish Literature,* I (New York, 1849), 241-242.

1

When Zifar's instructions are finished, Roboán the younger son announces that he will set out in the world to seek his fortune. His story comprises the third section of the book —«Los hechos de Roboán». The quest motif is again present but in contrast to the first division there is no compelling reason why Roboán must leave home. The young knight experiences a number of exciting adventures which in some ways parallel those of his father yet have qualities which are different. Eventually Roboán marries the ruler of Galapia and becomes emperor of Triguida.

In the *Zifar* the reader seems to be dealing with at least four separate literary entities (prologue, Zifar's story, the *Castigos* section, and Roboán's adventures) which have only a tenuous relation to one another. Each of the three major sections is in itself somewhat amorphous because the main line of action is usually complicated by a number of *exempla* and stylistic involvements.

Critics have for the most part agreed with Charles Philip Wagner who, in his study of the sources of the *Zifar*, warned straightaway that «we must not look for unity» in the work.[3] María Rosa Lida de Malkiel expressed this idea even more sharply when she called the book «...un no logrado maridaje de narración didáctica y de novela caballeresca».[4] Since the major divisions of the *Zifar* appear to be placed together without reason and as the moral and chivalric themes of the romance seem to play against one another irrationally, the critic is tempted to agree with Mrs. Lida de Malkiel's assessment. The reader could readily dismiss the work as no more than a stylistic and thematic potpourri hurriedly conceived and badly written.

Students of medieval literature, particularly those concerned with Old and Middle English, have realized that modern canons of structure and organization are not always applicable to works done before the Renaissance. Critics such as D. W. Robertson have suggested that criteria based upon literary formulizations of the period should be used when attempting to understand and evaluate a medieval work of art. Such arguments can prove very helpful in regard to Old Spanish literature.

The first critic to find a kind of unity in the *Zifar* was Justina Ruiz de Conde in her work *El amor y el matrimonio secreto en los libros de caballerías*. She noted that the two adventure segments of the first major division and «Los hechos de Roboán» have a similar structure —a supernatural episode is sandwiched between more realistic events in all three.[5] Roger Walker has continued this line of investigation and has encountered a number of motifs which occur in the same order in the adventure portions.[6] Walker describes an organization which is very similar to what has been called the «interlace mode» in medieval literature.[7]

The interlace mode allows the writer to weave together themes and motifs

[3] «The Sources of the *Caballero Cifar*», *RH*, X (1903), 6.
[4] *La idea de la fama en la edad media castellana* (México-Buenos Aires, 1952), 259.
[5] *El amor y el matrimonio secreto en los libros de caballerías* (Madrid, 1948), 46-57.
[6] «The Unity of *El Libro del Cavallero Zifar*», *BHS*, XLII (1965), 149-159.
[7] See Eugène Vinaver, *Form and Meaning in Medieval Romance* (Modern Humanities Research Association Presidential Address, 1966) and John Leyerle, «The Interlace Structure of *Beowulf*», *UTQ*, XXXVII (1967-1968), 1-17.

so as to establish a certain atmosphere of meaning and suggestion. The author may have little or no interest in the temporal relationship which exists between these ideas. The result is a work in which certain threads appear and disappear according to a pattern which may not always appear to be logical.

Certainly Walker has demonstrated that such an interwoven design exists in the *Zifar*. In addition it seems likely that the surface plane in the romance, the adventures of Zifar and his family, may suggest a secondary stratum. It is important to emphasize, however, that if such a stratum is defined as allegorical, the term must be taken in a special sense.

Normally medieval allegory suggests a *quid pro quo* construction in which the surface plane is merely an artificial service vehicle used to signal a series of hidden meanings. The primary layer has no significance of its own and may, to use the medieval example, be discarded as a worthless shell once the sweet kernel beneath has been found. Figural or typological allegory, the «allegory of the theologians» is something far different. Here the exterior stratum has a basic meaning of its own, valuable even if a reader were unable to see or appreciate any secondary connotations which it might have. But in line with a very ancient world-view all reality has to reflect the inscrutable mind of God in some way. Thus to many medievals the very historicity of a surface plane would imply the existence of another meaning co-existing with it.

My principal concern in this study is with this secondary stratum. The author of the *Zifar* has placed in the work a number of indications that the reader should view the life of the hero in two ways: first, as a true adventure story with a meaning which should be apparent to any reader; second, as one pole of a figural construction. I believe that the adventures of Zifar and Roboán fulfil a typological formula which begins in the Old Testament, is modified and given its strongest emphasis in the life of Christ, and which must recur in the lives of certain devout Christians until the end of time.

This spiritual plane, while in no way detracting from the reality, meaning and importance of the primary level, is an essential complement to it. The outline of this metaphysical plan may well prescribe the pattern which the author followed in choosing and aligning his «historical» episodes. The surface stratum can be understood alone. I believe, however, that the meaning of the work is much richer and more interesting if both planes can be taken together.

CHAPTER ONE

THE *ZIFAR* AS «VISION»

Those who followed Christ were aware, as the pagans had been before them, that they did not understand the physical and spiritual world. Yet, they had faith in the axiom given by St. Paul that they might attempt to perceive reflections of God's true order «as through a glass darkly».[1] The Almighty had woven the explanation of his grand design into nature, history and the Bible and had hidden it under a mantle of signs and semblances. The secret of every man's fate lay figured in the form of the universe.

> Omnis mundi creatura
> quasi liber et pictura
> nobis est in speculum,
> nostrae vitae, nostrae sortis
> nostri status, nostrae mortis
> fidele signaculum.[2]

Naturally scholars were interested in reading this «book» and in explaining to their fellow men the wisdom they found there. St. Paul had pointed the way to them with his example of the mirror. Reflections of divine meaning could be glimpsed by man in configurations intelligible to him in his fallen state. If nature and history were taken as these configurations, further interpretation would be necessary for the average Christian since such natural phenomena did not always appear to suggest philosophical or theological truths.

[1] *I Cor.*, 13.12.
[2] Alan of Lille, quoted in F. J. E. Raby, *A History of Christian-Latin Poetry* (Oxford, 1953), 355.

St. Augustine had implied that the verbal sign, particularly the aenigma, was the best way to express realities which were obscure and difficult to understand. [3] Marcia Colish explains the thinking of the Bishop of Hippo in the following manner: «An aenigma, like any other figure of speech, and like speech itself, is designed to communicate information. Its built-in difficulties thus enhance, rather than reduce, its expressive power. In attempting to convey the infinite incomprehensibility of God, then, an aenigma is a most suitable *vox significans rem*». [4] St. Augustine's belief in the importance of verbal communication was to dominate the entire Middle Ages. That Juan Manuel accepted verbal signs as capable of giving man an adequate understanding of God's mysteries is suggested in Chapter 34 of the *Libro del cavallero et del escudero* where he warns knights not to contemplate and dwell upon the problems of faith too much lest they damn themselves through doubt. «Ca la sotileza les faze pensar muchas cosas, et por la mengua de la letradura non pueden saber la verdat conplidamente como es.» [5] The implication is that «letradura», the understanding of verbal signs, can aid the Christian in understanding the ways of God.

Likewise the kind of verbal sign utilized was to be figurative and aenigmatic rather than literal. At the beginning of the first part of the *Conde Lucanor* Juan Manuel says that he does not wish to write the work in the «obscure» manner because then the work would be too difficult for the reader who was not «sotil». «Et porque [a] muchos omnes las cosas sotiles non les caben en los entendimientos, porque non las entienden bien, non toman plazer en leer aquellos libros, nin aprender lo que es escripto en ellos.» [6] In the second part, however, he decides, because of criticism, to return to the use of aenigma in his work. «Et porque don Jayme, señor de Xérica, que es uno de los omnes del mundo que yo más amo et por ventura non [amo] a otro tanto commo a él, me dixo que querría que los mis libros fablassen más oscuro, et me rogó que si algund libro feziesse, que non fuesse tan declarado. Et so çierto que esto me dixo porque él es tan sotil et tan de buen entendimiento, et tiene por mengua

[3] Marcia L. Colish, *The Mirror of Language* (New Haven, 1968), 79.
[4] *Ibid.*, See also Walter Ong, «Wit and Mystery», *Spec,* 22 (1947), 337.
[5] *Obras de don Juan Manuel,* ed. José María Castro y Calvo and Martín de Riquer I (Clásicos Hispánicos; Barcelona, 1955), 31.
[6] *El Conde Lucanor,* ed. José Manuel Blecua (Madrid, 1969), 51.

de sabiduría fablar en las cosas muy llana et declaradamente.»[7] The scholar may judge don Jaime's criticism in one or other of two ways: he may decide that don Jaime was merely insisting that Juan Manuel follow an established literary tradition; or he may think that don Jaime preferred to have moral wisdom passed to the reader in a form which in some manner resembled the inscrutable ways of the Creator. Most of the examples in the second and third parts of the *Conde Lucanor* are short conundrums which do probably contain excellent thoughts once they are properly understood. «Lo mucho es para mucho; mucho sabe [qui] en lo mucho faz mucho por lo mucho; lo poco dexa por lo mucho. Por mengua non pierde.»[8] Doubtless there is a kind of conceptualistic play here; also there may be an attempt to imitate in human terms the strange way in which God's creation seems to reveal and yet at the same time shield its message.

The reader can contemplate an aenigma such as the one above and he may eventually unravel its hidden meaning. But in a long work which consists of a great number of such riddles interlaced with symbols, exposition becomes very improbable if not impossible. In fact, it seems doubtful that the writers who composed such pieces had any desire that their readers be able to interpret them systematically. It is foolish to contend that a work like the *Divine Comedy*, the *Vida de Santa Oria* or the *Zifar* could be didactic in a catechistic sense. An *exemplum* such as those found in the *Libro de los gatos* or the *Libro de los enxiemplos por A.B.C.* presents a message, often clothed in allegory, which should be clear to any man having average intelligence. On the other hand a person seeking instruction in the tenets of the Christian faith would learn very little directly from the *Divine Comedy* although he might intuit a great deal.

A literary work such as the *Divine Comedy* must be a kind of intermediary exposition, a *speculum*, which allows the human intellect a glimpse of the outline of things beyond. Juan Manuel has perhaps given us a name for this literary elucidation. At the beginning of the *Libro de los estados* he tells us that he has used a somewhat artificial structure in the book because «los homes non pueden tambien entender las cosas por otra manera

---

[7] *Ibid.*, 263.
[8] *Ibid.*, 276.

7.

como por algunas semejanzas...» [9] In the *Libro de los estados* he is treating a series of rather straightforward problems. He presents these problems in a series of discussions which take place between the young prince Johas and the knight Turin and later the philosopher Julio. Juan Manuel has taken some variety of the Buddha legend and has used it as a frame to encapsulate and give form to his philosophical debate. *Semejanzas* here can be understood as the discussions which develop as a direct result of the use of the frame tale.

Later in the *Libro de los estados* the master of Peñafiel suggests that *semejanzas* should also be employed to explain much more complex matters. «... debedes saber que por razon que los homes somos envueltos en esta carnalidat gravosa, non podemos entender las cosas sotiles spirituales sinon por algunas semejanzas»; [10] Moses, he says, was faced with this problem when he needed to present God's laws to the Israelites. «Por eso lo puso estorialmente por tales palabras que lo entendiesen los homes somos de gruesa manera...» (347). Juan Manuel is saying that Moses interpreted God's plan to the Children of Israel in the form of *semejanzas*—stories which suggested in earthly terms the essence of divine meaning. In line with the Augustinian tradition the *semejanza* would be literary and it would also have to be conceived within the symbolic or aenigmatic mode.

When Juan Manuel spoke of a *semejanza* as a mirror for «las cosas sotiles spirituales», he cannot have been thinking of light allegories of the order of the tortoise and the hare which serve as an example of the virtues of steady labor versus wasteful speed. Even the allegorical correspondences of the Introduction to the *Milagros* of Berceo imply no truths which would merit the term «subtle». The episode is inviting because of its freshness and because of the charming images of nature presented there. Surely, however, everything that Berceo explains for us is quite basic and comprehensible to all Christians.

The *semejanza* as an earthly reflection of «cosas sotiles spirituales» seems apropos for those works which utilize the symbolic mode in order to suggest deep truths about the human condition. Such a *semejanza* is not an allegory but a *figura*. No systematic exegesis of this type of creation would ever be possible because

---

[9]   ed. Pascual de Gayangos, *BAE*, 51 (reprint, Madrid, 1941), 282.
[10] *Ibid.*, 347.

it alludes to a plane of reality which can be only glimpsed by
human understanding. The literary work is the «glass» which
St. Paul promised to Christians as a means for partial comprehension of God's truth while still in this life. The meaning of
the work reflects in human terms certain divine truths which
eternally exist on a superior plane. The word «darkly» in the
King James Version is a good adverb for implying the im-
perfect reception by the sinner of the image carried in the
mirror [11].

Perhaps the best synonym for *semejanza* —that is, an extended
verbal aenigma expressing metaphysical truths— may be found
in William Blake's term «vision». [12] Blake interprets «vision»
in the sense in which I think it to be applicable to medieval
figural allegory in his work *A Vision of the Last Judgment.*

> The Last Judgment is not Fable or Allegory but Vision   Fable
> or Allegory are a totally distinct & inferior kind of Poetry.   Vision
> or Imagination is a Representation of what Eternally Exists. Really
> & Unchangeably.   Fable or Allegory is Formd by the daughters
> of Memory. Imagination is Surrounded by the daughters of Inspi-
> ration who in the aggregate are calld Jerusalem... Fable is Allegory
> but what Critics call The Fable is Vision itself... The Hebrew

[11] I prefer to use the words of the King James Version rather than those of the
Vulgate because the 17th century translators of the Bible were in many respects
still medieval in their thinking. Thus the metaphor which they have chosen of «seeing in a glass darkly» is probably very close to expressing the manner in which the
medieval understood what St. Paul had said. The Latin is very terse: «Videmus
nunc per speculum in aenigmate...» Perhaps the best, exact translation of this phrase
should be: «We now see by means of a mirror, that is, in aenigma.» The translators
of the King James Version managed to merge beautifully the concepts of «mirror»
and «aenigma».

[12] I do not hope, of course, to imply any sort of link or correspondence between
the thinking of Juan Manuel or the author of the *Zifar* in the 14th century and
that of William Blake some five hundred years later. It does seem possible, however,
that an understanding of medieval works which are meant to symbolize or suggest
another plane of meaning can perhaps be gotten by studying the ideas of later writers
who utilized similar modes of expression. One might say with Jung that there are
only a certain number of ways of approaching any given human condition. Certainly
this would be true in regard to literary problems. Thus the solution which Dante
found for suggesting metaphysical truths within the context of human experience
might not be too far from that employed by Blake, particularly since both writers
were searching for a means of implying the great verities of the Christian God. Medieval authors unfortunately did not tend to be introspective in the few lines which
they occasionally penned about their work. Dante, for example, disposes of the
vast problem of the 4 senses of interpretation in the *Convivio* (II, i) in what can
be no more than 3 or 4 pages. The modern critic is left to infer the rest, as it
were, from «between the lines». Thus I offer my explanation of a parallelism
between Juan Manuel's *semejanza* and Blake's «vision» as an illustration which
I hope may prove to be thought-provoking. I do not ask that it be taken as
absolute.

> Bible & the Gospel of Jesus are not Allegory but Eternal Vision
> or Imagination of All that Exists... [13]

Northrop Frye explains Blake's meaning here by saying that
«A visionary creates, or dwells in, a higher spiritual world in
which the objects of perception in this one have become trans-
figured and charged with a new intensity of symbolism». [14]
Blake implies that there are two kinds of allegory, one «debased...
against which there is a reasonable and well-founded prejudice...»,
the other, «... a genuine allegory without which no art can be
fully understood». [15] Frye means in this explanation that the
true artist who senses the reality behind the façade of the physical
world creates (or finds) a symbolic play of art which faithfully
reproduces or reflects this reality. This presentation must be
rooted in and derived from events which take place in the everyday world.

This explanation serves well for works, such as those of Blake,
which are filled with symbolic configurations. The same idea
can certainly help us to understand the *Divine Comedy*. It is
not immediately clear, however, how the term «vision» could
be applicable to a book such as the *Zifar* in which the incidence
of symbolism seems to be much lower than in the *Commedia*
and where for the most part the plane of action is never far
removed from reality.

Angus Fletcher has made further observations about the
meaning of Blake's «vision». [16] «The vision, furthermore, is not
always visual. It appears that any temporal moment of particular
intensity can serve as a symbol of the center, or, putting it another
way, just as space is 'sacred space' in the Temple, so time is
'sacred time' in the Temple, while we can sometimes be shown
a moment of sacred time without any of the spatial trappings
that go to make up a proper temple.» [17] A «symbol of the center»
for Fletcher is «a temple or indeed any sacred place to which the
hero is drawn and in which he receives his initiation into the
vision of his true destiny». [18] Fletcher says that there are many

---

[13] *The Poetry and Prose of William Blake,* ed. David V. Erdman (Garden City,
N. Y., 1965), 544.
[14] *Fearful Symmetry: A Study of William Blake* (reprint, Princeton, 1969), 8.
[15] *Ibid.,* 10.
[16] *Allegory* (Ithaca, N. Y., 1964).
[17] *Ibid.,* 351.
[18] *Ibid.,* 350.

such «visions» in the *Quijote*, such as the episode in the Cave of Montesinos or the numerous happenings that take place at inns. He takes as his best example of the phenomenon, however, the episode in Melville's *Moby Dick* which immediately precedes the final encounter with the great white whale. Here in a very few lines the reader is given his deepest understanding of the meaning of Captain Ahab's quest. Yet, nothing at all really happens. Captain Ahab simply stands upon the deck and gazes into the water a moment while sensing the clear air and the «winsome sky». This tranquil setting evinces from him the most beautiful and moving thoughts of the entire work which prepare us for the cataclysmic events to follow.

Such instances of «vision» are a kind of sudden awareness when the character and the reader as well momentarily understand a transcendental meaning which is fleetingly etched upon the surface of reality. It is an epiphany—a manifestation not of a god but of the timeless realm where that god dwells. Such a vision or epiphany can consist of the most trivial events which suddenly and inexplicably take on great significance for the character who is experiencing them. The tapping of snow on a windowpane lifts Gabriel Conroy out of his hotel room in Joyce's *The Dead* and momentarily makes him one with the universe. «His soul swooned slowly as he heard the snow falling through the universe and faintly falling, like the descent of their last end, upon all the living and the dead.» [19] Earlier in the work Gabriel, in his after-dinner speech, has entreated his listeners not to forget those who, though once famous in the world, have passed on. «... let us hope, at least, that in gatherings such as this we shall still speak of them with pride and affection, still cherish in our hearts the memory of those dead and gone great ones whose fame the world will not willingly let die.» [20] The fellowship of the dinner table, the moralizing tone of the discourse, and the *camaraderie* which Joyce makes a subject of Gabriel's speech, vaguely evoke the atmosphere of the Mass, particularly the Oblation of the Bread at the beginning of the Offertory and the Commemoration of the Dead in the Canon where the priest suggests the unity of all past, present, and future

[19] *Dubliners* (reprint, London, 1956), 256.
[20] *Ibid.*, 232.

Christians. [21]   But artistically the agent which finally accomplishes this oneness for Gabriel is the snow which covers finally and absolutely all the living and the dead just as it blankets on that night all of Ireland.   Obviously we, the readers, cannot really ever hope to feel and understand exactly what Gabriel Conroy felt and knew as he watched the snow falling «obliquely against the lamplight».   Joyce simply presents it to us.   We have to make of it what we will.   We might not even comprehend fully if it were happening to us.

> For most of us there is only the unattended
> Moment, the moment in and out of time,
> The distraction fit, lost in a shaft of sunlight.
> ... of music heard so deeply
> That it is not heard at all, but you are the music
> While the music lasts.
>
> (Dry Salvages)

This «moment», «vision» or epiphany is the sudden awareness that everything fits together in some strange, unfathomable way. Eliot links the whole process to Christianity by saying that «These are only hints and guesses...   The hint half guessed, the gift half understood, is Incarnation».

One wonders if at least one interpretation of «Incarnation» might be the artistic work which embodies and gives form to the «hint».   Obviously the «hint» could never be understood standing completely alone.   But in the context of a work of art, the writer might be able to put across to his reader an atmosphere which could allow him to intuit such a «gift half-understood». Fletcher explained «vision» as a moment of intellectual crescendo which quickly fell away.   Frye correctly saw, however, that this «vision» could well be a very long work in which a number of manifestations occur.   The extensive framework would be necessary in order to add depth and give perspective to the instances of high insight.

Frye also says that «the greater the work of art, the more

---

[21]   William York Tindall, *A Reader's Guide to James Joyce* (New York, 1959), points out that Joyce may have conceived *Ulysses* as a Mass: «...there is good reason for thinking the whole book a kind of Mass... 'Was Parish worthe thette mess'? *(Finnegans Wake...)* asks Joyce referring to *Ulysses*. His question, involving Esau and his mess of potage, combines Dublin (province or parish) and the Paris of Henry IV. Mess or *messe* is Mass» (138, n. 2). If Joyce did, indeed, look upon *Ulysses* as a kind of great communion or Mass, then it might not be unlikely that *The Dead*, an earlier creation, might also have involved the same idea.

completely it reveals the gigantic myth which is the vision of this world as God sees it, the outlines of that vision being creation, fall, redemption and apocalypse». [22] A work of art taken as this kind of «vision» would be like a religious rite or mystery such as that of the Greek Orthodox Church which takes place behind the iconostasis unviewed by the congregation. The faithful are unaffected by doubt for they know that God does not need their attention nor their complete understanding in order to perform His miracles.

I would suggest that the *Libro del Cavallero Zifar* is a *semejanza*, a «vision» which expresses the outline of creation, fall, redemption, and apocalypse. Many happenings in the work constitute a pole of a figural construction. The framework of the romance allows the reader to see in context that a relationship exists between an event in the life of the knight and something out of the great stream of sacred history.

Because both poles in a figure are real, it is necessary to take what happens in the *Zifar* as historically true. The comprehension, the *intellectus spiritualis*, as Auerbach calls it, [23] of a typological bond between something in the work and some transcendental happening is by no means the only intellectual exercise worthy of the reader's attention. The adventures of Zifar and his family have important meanings in themselves and deserve study. At the same time the reader has to be aware that the knight's actions do often allude to another plane as important for the soul as this present life is for the body.

If we do view and understand the *Zifar* in this manner, it is fatuous to attempt to explain it as an absolutely logical demonstration of any doctrine. The work seems to be concerned with certain basic tenets of the Christian faith. Yet if it is to be taken as «vision», the reader must remain aware that to a certain extent, he is to be always on the outside. He has to respect the work while attempting to intuit as well as he can the deep inspiration of faith which evinced it. He must hope that the book, as a work of art, can communicate to him the message and thought which the author intended—not directly in a logical manner but indirectly through the imagination.

[22] *Fearful Symmetry*, 108.
[23] Erich Auerbach, *Mimesis: The Representation of Reality in Western Literature* (reprint, Garden City, N. Y., 1957), 64.

CHAPTER TWO

LITURGY AND ALLEGORY

The adventures of Zifar and Roboán in *El libro del Cavallero Zifar* have meanings which transcend the normal functions of chivalry in that they illustrate basic Christian doctrine and experience. The story line on the surface has its own significance; at the same time it alludes to a secondary series of ideas. In order to follow what the author was attempting to explain, we must interpret both of the planes in his work. Obviously the secondary level will present the greater problem to the critic: he must first demonstrate that it does indeed exist, and secondly show adequately what it means. This kind of figural allegory which the author of the *Zifar* has used differs considerably from a point-by-point correspondence between two meanings. His subordinate plane is «real» and has relation to real phenomena. He connects it with reality and infuses it with veracity by using the liturgy of the Church as a backdrop against which to develop his primary and secondary levels.

The changing Church calendar constantly affects the mode of worship of the faithful. Any given day in the year can be significant to the Church either because it has been designated in honor of a saint or because it commemorates some occurrence important for the teachings of Christ. Saints' days are found throughout the year, but the great liturgical seasons, periods of time which recall the most signal events from the life of the Saviour, are grouped so as to leave a large portion of the calendar vacant. The seasonal Church year begins with Advent which leads up to Christmas, the birth of the Saviour. The Advent-Christmas phase ends with Epiphany on January 6 and there is a brief pause until Septuagesima Sunday when the Church

14

orients itself toward the somber exercises of Lent. Lent terminates with Holy Week and the joys of the Resurrection on Easter Day. There follow the «Fifty Days» during which the Church meditates on the meaning of the Resurrection and its implications for the eschatological needs of mankind. The end of the «Fifty Days» is Pentecost, the anniversary of the descent of the Holy Spirit upon the Apostles. After Pentecost the great and important liturgical seasons end, to begin again with the next Advent. There are, of course, short periods of importance for the Christian faith such as the September Ember Days, but the «commemoration» of those events which are of most basic importance for Christian life takes place between Advent and Pentecost.

The introduction to the Proper of the Season in the St. Andrew Daily Missal gives an excellent idea of what the Church sees in the great liturgical seasons.

> Every year from Advent to Pentecost she (i. e. the Church) causes us to celebrate the principal events of our Saviour's life, not as a mere commemoration, but to renew us by the application of the especial graces which the celebration of each event brings us. This living communication of the mysteries of Christ thus permeates our souls with an authentic Christian life, closely bound up with that of the Church. [1]

In essence the Church holds the same view of the liturgical seasons today as it did in the Middle Ages save for the indisputable fact that Protestantism and modern ideas of progress have tended to dull the great awareness and feeling for liturgical rite which must have existed among medieval Christians.

The Church, in celebrating annually the historical life of Jesus, is able to pour out upon her faithful again and again the saving grace which springs from the events of His life. What the modern has trouble understanding (and appreciating) is the manner in which this grace is received. For example the Church asks that her faithful, in order to acquire the benefits of the Easter communion, undergo the spiritual exercises of Lent which consist of self-denial, fasting, prayer, confession, and penance. These present-day practices do not seemingly evince the mood of anguish suggested in the Introit for Septuagesima:

[1] Dom Gaspar Lefebvre, *Saint Andrew Daily Missal* (Bruges, 1958), 3.

15

«The sorrows of death surrounded me, the sorrow of hell encompassed me: and in my affliction I called upon the Lord...» The celebration of the modern liturgy has become largely an intellectual experience so that the atmosphere which dictated the placing of verses from Psalm 17 at the beginning of Septuagesima, to mark and characterize it, is almost absent from the Church.

O. B. Hardison has demonstrated that the early medieval Church looked upon the events of the Easter cycle as though they were really happening again and as if the whole living community were there watching them. When Hardison speaks of Christians «prostrate at the foot of the cross on Good Friday» because of the death of the Saviour of the World which had occurred on that day, he is probably very close to the atmosphere of anguish and despair which characterized the moment during the Middle Ages. [2]

For medieval man the events of the liturgical year were real mysteries, not just in an intellectual sense but in an active one. The Middle Ages viewed the Church year as a real repetition of the Nativity, Passion, death, and Resurrection of Jesus, all of which implied personal and cosmic regeneration. [3] It was through his active participation in this process that the Christian received the bountiful saving grace of Christ. Scholars may still be debating whether the Church should accept the idea that Christ's Passion, death and Resurrection are actually made present when these events are commemorated. [4] The medieval Christian, however, was not concerned with the fine points of theological argument; he lived in a world caught between time and eternity in which the events which had made possible his salvation were played out again and again. [5]

The Hebraic idea of temporal movement was that the world had a definite beginning in time (the Creation) and that it was progressing toward a definite end (the Coming of the Messiah). The Church Fathers took this idea and changed it by making the

[2] O. B. Hardison, *Christian Rite and Christian Drama in the Middle Ages* (Baltimore, 1965), 130-131.
[3] Cf. Mircea Eliade, *The Myth of the Eternal Return* (New York, 1954), 130.
[4] See Josef A. Jungmann, *The Early Liturgy* (Notre Dame, Indiana, 1954), 161-162.
[5] This conception of eternal reality can be glimpsed even today in such spirituals as «Were you there when they crucified my Lord?» where the humble and unlearned Christian is so swept away by the force of Christ's Passion that it becomes, and is, real for him. See Lynn White Jr., «Christian Myth and Christian History», *JHI*, 3 (1942), 153.

life of Christ the mid-point between the Creation and the Second Coming. The belief in the constant cyclic repetition of every thing and every event, widely held among the Greeks and Romans, was relegated to the realm of nature. [6] It is possible that the Church, in an effort to reconcile pagan ideas of cyclic return with Christian doctrine, actually encouraged or at least tolerated the idea that the central events of Christ's life did recur mystically each year. [7] If Christ's body and blood of the Last Supper actually does appear on the altar—and it must be remembered that there was still argument about this as late as the 11th and 12th centuries— is it not equally logical that He annually is crucified, buried and resurrected? [8]

It seems likely that during the Middle Ages Christians believed that Christ's Passion was mystically repeated with each Easter season. They certainly accepted the idea that the particular force or «meaning» of an event out of Christ's life was most strongly felt at the time when the Church celebrated it on the liturgical calendar.

[6] John Baillie, *The Belief in Progress* (London, 1950), 66-67. Eliade says that «the circular movement that ensures the maintenance of the same things by repeating them, by continually bringing back their return, is the most immediate, the most perfect (and hence the most nearly divine) expression of that which, at the pinnacle of the hierarchy, is absolute immobility» (89n).

[7] St. Augustine in *City of God* XII, 13 and 17 argues vehemently against any idea of cyclic recurrence except in nature. St. Paul in Eph. 2.2ff had reminded Christians that they had no hope when they were pagans because they were held by their beliefs in the endless cycles. Nevertheless, the Church did institute the cyclical year which originated in the celebration of established events in Christ's life. The problem is how the Middle Ages viewed this cyclic repetition of redeeming history. It is possible that the ever-present archetypal idea of eternal recurrence crept back into Christian thinking so that at least in the popular mind the «reality» of past occurrences would be regenerated for the individual Christian through faith. He might then share in the «eternal *nunc*» (Eliade, 120) of God's timeless realm beyond history. Eliade believes that the Middle Ages were «dominated by the eschatological conception (in its two essential moments: the creation and the end of the world), complemented by the theory of cyclic undulation that explains the periodic return of events» (144).

[8] It was not until the Fourth Lateran Council of 1215 that the definition of the dogma of Transubstantiation was finally fixed. Hardison compares the ordinary of the Mass (that part which changes according to the date) in terms of absolute time versus cyclical time. The ordinary would represent a kind of «still point» at which all sacrifices of the Mass past, present, and future would be one and the same, while the proper is indicative of the annual cycle which changes for 365 days and then begins again (83-85). However, if popular sentiment in the Middle Ages imagined that the «truth» or «reality» of such past actions as Christ's death on the cross were recapitulated on Good Friday, then there would be no real difference between the «absolute» time of the Consecration-Last Supper and the recapitulated time of the Crucifixion-Adoration of the Cross on Good Friday. The Consecration-Last Supper would recur everyday in the Mass while the «reality» of the Crucifixion would be observed only once in the 365 day cycle.

17

For example Juan Manuel uses the same word *remembranza* [9] to describe the reason for the institution of the Sacrament of the Mass and for the singing of the hours of the Virgin on Saturday. «Otrosí, dexó este sancto sacramento porque fincasse en su remembrança...» «... et porque fincó en ella solamente toda la fe desde la hora que Jesucristo finó el viernes fasta el domingo que resucitó, por ende ordenó la sancta Eglesia que por remembranza de esto cantasen todos los sábados las horas de Santa María». [10] Juan Manuel must have believed that the Mass and the hours of the Virgin commemorated in much the same way the Last Supper and the sorrows of Mary. Both mystically recapitulated and made present the virtue and significance of the original event. The Christian could partake of the body of Christ at the communion and thus share in the continuing sacrifice, at one with the original sacrifice, by which he and all mankind could be saved. The chanting of the hours of the Virgin commemorated Mary's great devotion and reminded Christians of her powers of intercession.

It is essential, thus, when studying artistic works which have relation to the liturgy, to view the events of that liturgy not as mere historical re-enactments, but rather as «ways of participating in the rhythm, the very actuality, of the divine life». [11] The doing of the will of God is the most important duty of every Christian. The example and archetype of what obedience to God can accomplish was given in the actions of Christ, He whom every man must follow and imitate. To keep this example fresh, the Church, under figure of the daily office and Proper of the Season, constantly repeats and implies the life of Christ along

---

[9] The correct technical term for *remembranza* is *anamnesis* which begins at the words «unde et memores» in the Mass. *Anamnesis* is «...an objective memorial directed Godward, releasing Christ's personality and power afresh; it is the experience of a fellowship with Christ in His eternal sacrifice» (F. A. Brunner, «Anamnesis», *NCE*, I, 476).

[10] The first reference is from the *Quinta parte del libro de Conde Lucanor et de Patronio*, ed. José Manuel Blecua (Madrid, 1969), 289. The second is from Juan Manuel, *Libro de los estados*, ed. Pascual de Gayangos *BAE*, 51 (reprint, Madrid, 1941), 283. Another example of mystically recapitulated past time in a Church feast may be found in Berceo's *Vida de Santo Domingo de Silos*. St. Domingo tells other monks in the monastery that the king, queen, and bishop will be at the monastery in 4 days (505). On the appointed day the bishop is there but not the king and queen who are far away. The monks think that St. Domingo is insane. The holy man points out, however, that the day is the Incarnation when Christ entered Mary and they are the greatest of kings and queens. Thus in reality the king and queen, Christ and Mary, are present mystically in the monastery (511).

[11] Alan W. Watts, *Myth and Ritual in Christianity* (New York, 1954), 25.

18

with those Old Testament happenings which alluded to Jesus as well as those events promised for the moment of His Second Coming. The medieval Christian saw the entire spectrum of sacred history unfolding constantly year after year in the practices and observances of the Church. He viewed the Church year not as mere allusion to totally past events, nor to ones yet to come, but as the active representation in his life of the ever-present force of those events.

It seems likely that a medieval writer, keenly aware of what the constant change in the Church liturgy signified, might have made use of this significance when he constructed a literary work which itself would unfold through time in linear fashion. Dante begins his *Inferno* on Good Friday surely to avail himself of the fabric of meaning which Christian history posits upon that day through figural «rememoration» in the liturgy. For the modern student who first approaches the *Divine Comedy*, the time setting is only one of many incidental details which must be taken into account when reading the work. Probably he would see nothing wrong in stating that Dante could have begun his poem on Christmas Eve or All Saints or any other great feast of the Church. But for medieval man and for anyone aware of what Dante was attempting to do, it would be inconceivable that the poet's journey should have taken place at any other point in the year. The meaning of the work and the meaning of the season harmonize completely—to separate them would destroy the import of the poem.

Chandler Post in his *Mediaeval Spanish Allegory* notes the «scrupulous observance of the date» as a «commonplace of mediaeval allegory», [12] but says that it is due to a desire for realism and verisimilitude. I would suggest that the giving of the date in a medieval work (which is almost always according to the Church calendar) was done many times for more important reasons. Just as the Good Friday setting lends an atmosphere of ritual and sacramental associations to the beginning of the *Divine Comedy*, so another date on the Church calendar might serve the same function for a poet or writer who wished to use it. [13] If a medieval author were composing a work in which

[12] Chandler Rathfon Post, *Mediaeval Spanish Allegory* (Harvard Studies in Comparative Literature 4; Cambridge, Mass., 1915), 122.
[13] It is interesting to note that T. Anthony Perry in his perceptive study *Art*

he hoped to illuminate artistically certain verities important to him (which in the majority of cases would have been related to the tenets of the Catholic faith), he would find in the liturgy a pattern, or better a frame, against which to bond his story. By placing his ideas against a pre-existing and recognized time-system, itself heavy with meaning, he could incorporate into his work an atmosphere suggested by that system without having actually to build up this plane himself. [14]

My thesis is, thus, that in many medieval works of literature the writer used the liturgical calendar as a backdrop against which to play out the action of his story. Because of the wide influence of the Church he could have expected his readers to be aware of the significance of each liturgical event (often no doubt in a very dramatic sense).

The Christian allegorical worldview saw all creation as analogically similar in some fashion to the Creator. [15] Supported

---

and Meaning in Berceo's Vida de Santa Oria (Yale Romanic Studies, Second Series 19; New Haven and London, 1968) at first accepts Post's reasoning in regard to why Berceo gave the exact date for the saint's three visions (50). Later in his work Perry admits that the setting of the visions within the Proper of the Saints might have other reasoning behind it which would dissociate it from concepts of linear time. «The cyclical view, on the other hand, seems more congenial to ethics than to knowledge, to didacticism rather than to discovery or experience for its own sake. For the didactic is based on the *notion of type* [italics mine] of the essential and periodic recurrence of experience and moral patterns» (123-124n). What seems possible is that Berceo (or the writer of the now lost life of St. Oria in Latin) might have artistically placed the date of her visions on saints' days whose office recounted events similar in tone to those experienced by the girl Oria. In the same manner the Cid is said to have died on Pentecost although it is unlikely that the poet actually knew the real date of his death. Pentecost is doubtless given so that the poet may imply to the reader that the great hero went to his reward on that feast of the Church which was traditionally associated with the glory of the afterlife. Bernard Levy in «Gawain's Spiritual Journey: *Imitatio Christi* in *Sir Gawain and the Green Knight*», *Annuale Medievale*, 6 (1965), says that the *Gawain* poet mentions St. Michael's feast day «because Gawain's coming ordeal will in some measure parallel Michael's...» (87). F. W. Locke, *The Quest for the Holy Grail* (Stanford, Calif., 1960), observes that the mention of the Vigil of Pentecost in the *Queste* at one level merely defines the time of action on the Christian calendar: «But it has another and more important function... The action of the narrative flows from the images chosen to support it, which have an independent existence outside the *Queste* in the liturgical celebration of the Church» (43).

[14] As an example in modern literature one might mention William Faulkner's *The Sound and the Fury* where undoubtedly the Good Friday-Easter time setting is full of significance for the work as a whole.

[15] «At the basis of all medieval thought is the concept of *analogy*. All things have been created according to the law of analogy, in virtue of which they are, in various degrees, manifestations of God, images, vestiges, or shadows of the creator...» (Otto Von Simson, *The Gothic Cathedral,* New York, 1956, 54). St. Bonaventure presents the same idea in another form: «totus mundus est sicut unum speculum plenum luminibus praesentibus divinam sapientiam, et sicut carbo, effundens lucem»

by biblical texts such as Psalm 19.1—«The heavens declare the glory of God; and the firmament sheweth his handywork» [16]— medieval man searched for God's design in every naturally occurring phenomenon. [17] The principal expression of the Almighty's scheme for the universe was the Bible where all truth and knowledge could be found. Unfortunately the meaning placed in the Holy Scriptures by God often lay veiled in metaphors and symbols. St. Paul in I Cor. 13.12 and II Cor. 3.18 had, with his famous phrase of «seeing through a glass darkly», suggested to the exegete a procedure for seeking and explaining the significance implied by the surface figures. From the time of the Alexandrine Fathers, the Church had proceeded to try and comprehend the image in the mirror in the best possible manner so that it might teach and spread true doctrine.

Now the Bible was conceived as being God's work and thus written by Him. Medieval men of course realized that there had been in many cases an intermediary scribe who had copied down the real historical events. But they believed that this scribe, guided by the Holy Spirit, had recorded the happening, adhering to the letter of truth as fully as it was possible for a human being to do. The Gospels were «written» by God in the same sense that any other series of historical occurrences or religious doctrines were «written» or produced by him. [18] The scribe did the actual writing; but he copied down faithfully the history of events which had really happened.

This manner of looking at the composition of the Bible led the Middle Ages to a very particular way of viewing history. History had something to say because it, like the Bible, was «written by God». Man could learn from studying history (or the outcome of historical sequences) if he knew how to interpret it correctly and, more important, if he had an exact record. If there were errors in his rendition, then the errors, obviously of human origin and not divinely ordained, would

(quoted in Etienne Gilson, *The Philosophy of St. Bonaventure*, trans. Illtyd Trethowan and F. J. Sheed, London, 1938, 230).

[16] The same idea is also present in Isaiah 40.22 and Romans 1.19-20.

[17] «As the Middle Ages progressed, other things are significant also, so that creation itself is an allegorical book revealing beneath the 'literal' or visible surface of objects 'the invisible things of God' (Rom. 1.20)» (D. W. Robertson, *A Preface to Chaucer*, Princeton, 1962, 296). See also Von Simson, 53.

[18] As in Hebrews 5.9 where Christ is spoken of as «the author of eternal salvation».

invalidate the sacramental value of the history in that it would no longer be a true reflection of God's order.

Juan Manuel wrote the *Libro de las armas* at the request of one Frey Johan Alonso so that «podemos fazer cavalleros yo et míos fijos legítimos non seyendo nos cavalleros...»[19] The arming of a knight was an elaborate, almost liturgical, ceremony having close connections with Church ritual. The knighting of a member of the ruling family, those chosen to be vicars of God on earth, would have signal importance as a prototype for other occasions since, once conceived of as historical fact, it could be viewed as part of the cosmic design of the universe. So Juan Manuel is most concerned with the validity of what he is writing as a historical event.

> ... et así non vos do yo testimonio que bi todas estas cosas, mas oýlas a personas que eran de crer. Et non lo oý todo a una persona, mas oý unas cosas a una persona et otras a otras, et ayuntando lo que oý a los unos et a los otros con razón, ayunté estos dichos, (et por mi entendimiento entendí que passara todo el fecho en esta manera que vos yo porné aquí por escripto) que fablan de las cosas que passaran et así contesçe en los que fablan las scripturas: toman de lo que fallan en un logar et acuerdan en lo que fallan en otros lugares et de todo fazen una razón... [20]

Juan Manuel backs up his method of gathering and writing history by saying that he has been most careful to try and garner the truth by a method of comparison and contrast. According to the medieval point of view, he or anyone else would have been justified in finding a secondary plane of meaning in the events which he described, because, being true history, they would have to reflect the mind of God in some way.

Starting with the Bible, the exegete extended his eye over every facet of the created world. The Middle Ages felt justified in seeing God in the processes of history, in nature and in every other naturally occurring phenomenon.[21] Modern scholars

---

[19] *Obras de Juan Manuel*, 75.

[20] *Ibid.*, 75-76. It would be interesting to assume that the word «scripturas» refers to the Holy Scriptures. More likely Juan Manuel has the chronicles in mind. In either case, the idea is the same. He is of necessity forced to allow the writer some leeway in gathering his material.

[21] «In accordance with this system of symbolic interpretation any event, provided it had *actual objective* meaning (a necessary prerequisite) in the material world, might be studied in its relations to the universal pattern...» (Sister Teresa C. Goode, *Gonzalo de Berceo, El Sacrificio de la Misa*, Washington, D. C., 1933, 33). Johan

realize that the liturgy, while evolving over several centuries, was the creation of men, albeit inspired ones. Medieval exegetes saw the rites of the Church as something conceived by God and frozen into the fabric of history by His hand. It mattered little how the process had come about; it was part of the cosmic plan and had to have more than a surface meaning. By the 9th century there existed systematic treatises on all aspects of the liturgy which explained to Christians God's sacramental plan in all its intricacy. [22] The great explicators of the liturgical forms, such as Amalarius of Metz and Durandus of Mende, [23] viewed the rites of the Church as representing God's redemptive plan in the same way that the Bible or the universe reflects the divine order.

The most rudimentary allegory is no more than a point-by-point system in which one group of things or events is used to represent another group. [24] Such an artificial contrivance is common in the Middle Ages. The best example in early Spanish literature is the Introduction to the *Milagros* of Berceo where the poet sets up an elaborate scene which is nothing more than a decorative way of expressing certain truths about human life as he saw it. This is the «allegory of the poets». [25] Berceo makes

Chydenius shows how the capture of Jerusalem in the First Crusade and the events taking place afterwards were viewed by commentators and chroniclers as fulfilments of events prophesied in the Old Testament as well as being foreshadowings of things to happen when the Christian reached the heavenly city (*The Typological Problem in Dante,* Helsingfors, 1958, 77-86). For nature see John Scotus Erigena, *PL,* 122, 129.

[22] Goode, 27.

[23] Amalarius, *PL,* 105, 815-1360. Durandus wrote the *Rationale divinorum officiorum* (Antwerp, 1614).

[24] The best comprehensive study of the phenomenon of medieval allegory is that of Robertson, *A Preface to Chaucer.* Robertson's method and beliefs have been much criticized. For a listing of many of the critics and a very effective and sensible answer to them see A. Leigh Deneef, «Robertson and the Critics», *CR,* 2 (1967-68), 217. The work which probably comes closest to explaining how medieval allegory functioned in the romances is Rosemund Tuve, *Allegorical Imagery* (Princeton, 1966). An excellent presentation of the tenets of medieval symbolism is Johan Chydenius, *The Theory of Medieval Symbolism* (Helsingfors, 1960).

[25] «If we take the allegory of the *Divine Comedy* to be the allegory of poets (as Dante understood that allegory in the *Convivio),* then we shall be taking it as a construction in which the literal sense ought always to be expected to yield another sense because the literal is only a fiction devised to express a second meaning. In this view the first meaning, if it does not give another, *true* meaning, has no excuse for being. Whereas, if we take the allegory of the *Divine Comedy* to be the allegory of the theologians, we shall expect to find in the poem a first, literal meaning presented as meaning which is not fictive but true, because the words which give that meaning point to events which are seen as historically true» (Charles Singleton, «Dante's Allegory», *Spec.,* 25, 1950, 81). Singleton derives his understanding of

no claim that the events which he describes are really true; he expects the reader to understand them as creations of his own mind. Thus if the figures are the inventions of the poet, then the meanings inherent in them can only be meanings which were clear and comprehensible to him. If he were wrong in his understanding, his configurations would necessarily reflect his error. The meaning placed into a work by a writer had to be absolutely true for the reader only if he chose to follow the course prescribed to him by the text. In contrast the meaning placed into the Bible, history and the universe by God had always to be valid since God as the ultimate source of all meaning could never be in error. The exegete only had to find the significance and interpret it correctly.

Charles Singleton and those who have followed him have rightly stated that we must view the action of the *Divine Comedy* as true. We have to accept that Dante really made such a journey and that the events which he described from this journey happened. Robert Hollander, the latest of those critics who view the *Comedy* as reality, insists that Dante wrote in «imitation of God's way of writing». [26] Hollander admits that if the Florentine poet did compose in the manner of the «allegory of the theologians» he would have had to ignore St. Thomas Aquinas' statement that only God is capable of accommodating a thing to a meaning. For Hollander «The *Commedia* is a poem, and not a history; but it is a poem unlike most other poems in that it takes itself as history, and even as that kind of history which would be found in a 'new chapter in Scripture'». [27] Now the kind of «real» allegory which exists in the *Commedia* is typological or figural, that is, it shows the relations of events in the work to other manifestations of God's eternal meanings in history. [28] Typology

the two kinds of allegory not only from what Dante himself said but also from the remarks of St. Thomas Aquinas in the *Summa* I, i 10. Of course this «allegory of the poets» is much the same as or a continuation of the allegorical method of the Stoics, Philo, and the School of Alexandria. See Chydenius, *Typological Problem in Dante,* 24-28: «The immediate sense of the words lacked any value of its own and only served as a means of expressing the spiritual matter which the author wished to present» (28).

[26] *Allegory in Dante's Commedia* (Princeton, 1969), 23.

[27] *Ibid.,* 49, n. 39.

[28] The basic study on typology is Erich Auerbach, «Figura», in *Scenes from the Drama of European Literature* (New York, 1959), 54. Auerbach points out that figural interpretation and «allegory» differ only in the valid historicity of both the sign and what it signifies in the former. D. W. Foster agrees with Auerbach on the difference between the figural and the allegorical approach and finds the figural

connects two «real» happenings—two occurrences of absolute validity. Dante was certainly capable of writing a great poem, but he most certainly *was not* capable of creating reality, which is the province of God and God alone. Thus if Dante only «imitated» God's way of working, no matter how one twists and mangles logic, he is still accommodating only *words* to meaning because he cannot create. If he had believed that he held this power, doubtless the Church would have judged him either insane or heterodox. Since typology is the explanation of a relationship which exists between two separate events in history, no human can do more than point out that such a connection exists. He cannot gratuitously create one of the poles himself and then claim that he has come upon a valid figural bond.

Martin Stevens has criticized O. B. Hardison's contention that the Mass and liturgy (such as the Lenten rite) are drama. [29] In Stevens' view there is a very real and essential difference between the two forms. What happens in the Church is a ritualistic recapitulation of an eternal *nunc* which has sacramental significance for mankind. The Church-related drama of the Middle Ages is only a secondary imitation of events out of sacred history performed for didactic or aesthetic purposes. The dividing line for Stevens between rite and play is the liturgical accuracy involved. As long as a trope adheres strictly to the liturgy, then it would be viewed as rite with connotations of mystic reality about it. When additional material is added to the trope which dissociates it from liturgical context, it becomes drama and its relation to absolute meaning is one of analogy.

One would have to make the same statement about typological relationships in Dante's *Commedia* if the events in the work are

method exemplified in the *Auto de los reyes magos* («Figural Interpretation and the *Auto de los reyes magos*», *RR*, 58, 1967, 3-11). A. C. Charity, *Events and their Afterlife* (Cambridge, 1966), reminds us that the most basic principle of typology is that the important thing is the events, the *res gesta* which surround the character or what he accomplishes. It is not the *persona* himself. He can form a typological bond with another figure only if his circumstances resemble those of the other person. (109, n. 1). R. W. Frank has perceived that this is indeed the case in medieval literature: «A personification is thus allegoric by its action and not because it represents something different from itself (which it does not); it is the action which carries the secondary meaning, which differs from the one apparent». («The Art of Reading Medieval Personification Allegory», *ELH*, 20, 1953, 242-243). Although Frank does not mention the word «typology», I think that it is clear that this is what he has in mind.

[29] A Paper delivered at the University of Western Michigan Conference on Medieval Studies on May 20, 1970.

artificial, that is, if they were created in the imagination of the poet. The typology present would be one analogous to that true variety indicated by exegetes and students of sacred history. The *Commedia* would be «play» —imitative of the truth of God's universe but certainly not sharing in it in the same way that the Bible, nature or history does. This, I believe, is a valid possibility. However, Dante's statements in the Letter to Can Grande and, indeed, the very mood of the *Commedia* seem to suggest that the poet looked upon his work as more than mere «imitation». The author of the *Zifar* claims historical validity for his work and thus implies (as we shall see in the next chapter) that real ties may be seen to exist between happenings in the *Zifar* and those of history. The medieval writer must have known of a method which allowed him to express himself in creative terms related to valid typological procedure.

T. Anthony Perry suggests that «A good access to symbolism in *Santa Oria* is to accept Berceo's constant assertion that the story is historically true». [30] Berceo's thesis is quite acceptable to us because, after all, the *vita* is the life of a saint who actually existed and without doubt the Latin model from which the poet copied was read on Oria's feast day. Because of its use within the liturgy, it would have had to satisfy Stevens' requirement that it be taken as mystic truth. Thus an exegete could have justifiably shown the existence of typological bonds between events in Oria's life and other occurrences out of sacred history.

Jean Leclercq has demonstrated, however, that medieval hagiographers often borrowed details from the lives of well-known saints in order to fill out and make more distinctive the *vita* of a holy personage which they might have been commissioned to write. [31] A. C. Charity has demonstrated that from the earliest saints' lives a certain stylization may be noted which results from the writer's attempt to bring the life of the saint into conformity with that of his exemplar Jesus Christ. [32] Indeed a close examination of details in the life of St. Oria as written by Berceo shows that it is a mosaic of traditions garnered from numerous sources. [33]

[30] Perry, *Art and Meaning*, 95.
[31] *The Love of Learning and the Desire for God*, trans. Catharine Misrahi (New York, 1961), 202.
[32] See Footnote 11, Chapter 3.
[33] See my article «The Four 'Comings' of Christ in Gonzalo de Berceo's *Vida de Santa Oria*», *Spec* (in press).

If this is true and if Berceo were aware of it, and even more important, if he himself wove new motifs into the life of Oria as he found it (which I believe to be likely), why should he subsequently claim that the story was true? The answer tells us not only how such a fabricated saint's life could be accepted as valid even for liturgical purposes, but it also suggests how the creative writer such as the author of the *Zifar* or Dante could compose a piece within which absolute typological connections might be perceived.

In order to elucidate this problem I draw an example from the *vita* of the now obscure Spanish saints Facundus and Primitivus. [34] After enduring torture for their faith, the two are beheaded by their tormentors. The hagiographer tells us that *lac et sanguis* issued from their necks. The reader immediately thinks of the water and blood with their sacramental significance which poured from Christ's pierced side. The death of the two saints is an *imitatio* of that of the Saviour, but it is slightly varied in that water has been changed to milk and, of course, the part of the body is different. The hagiographer may have made the change so that the death of Facundus and Primitivus would, like that of St. Peter, not resemble Christ's Passion too closely. There is also perhaps a more concrete reason for the change to milk.

The feast day of SS. Facundus and Primitivus is November 27. The First Sunday in Advent is always November 27 if Advent runs the full four week cycle. When Advent had four weeks and the First Sunday thus coincided with the feast of SS. Facundus and Primitivus, the seasonal liturgy would doubtless have taken precedence and the two saints would only have been commemorated during the Mass. The first antiphon for Vespers for Advent I is Joel 3.18: «In illa die stillabunt montes dulcedinem, et colles fluent lac et mel, alleluia.» Since the majority of antiphons and responses in the Advent cycle are Old Testament verses which typologically point to Christ whose nearness is signaled in the liturgy, it is likely that the «montes» and «colles» might have been seen as a type of Christ on the cross while the milk and honey

---

[34] The life is given in *España Sagrada,* ed. Enrique Flórez, 34 (Madrid, 1784), 398. Flórez unfortunately does not give the date of the manuscript from which he took the life but says that it is a Gothic codex from the monastery of Cardeña (34, 318).

could have been understood as prefiguring the water and blood which in their turn signal the Sacraments of the altar. The possibility then occurs that the composer of the lives of Facundus and Primitivus reached back to an Old Testament prefigurement, brought before him in the liturgy for the First Sunday in Advent when it coincided with November 27, for the motif of the milk. There is very little difference etymologically between the *colles* of Joel and the *de collis* of the *vita*. If my interpretation is correct, we would have two motifs, one from the Old Testament prefigurement, the other from the Christ-pattern, both projected into the lives of two Christians who followed their Saviour in martyrdom.

The unknown writer who composed the life of SS. Facundus and Primitivus was not being dishonest when he appropriated motifs from the typological tradition for use in his *vita*. He may well have been following the rules of a genre, as Dom Leclercq believes, which allowed him to mix Isidorian *fabula* and *narratio* and then present the result as ritual truth. I feel that there is also another possibility. The verse from Joel, the death of Christ (the principal manifestation) and that of the two saints were reflections within history of one eternal truth which must rest at the still point with the Creator. The essence of this truth never alters nor does that of its imitation within the human sphere. But because circumstances do change with the movement of time, the form of the reflection has to differ from one moment to the next. Thus these three examples represent the same truth, but the configuration of that truth is different in each case. The hagiographer who realized that the Old Testament type and the New Testament era subfulfilment [35] do demonstrate the essence of something principally proven in the life of Christ could range wide for his material. He might, for artistic or aesthetic purposes, take a metaphor from the Old Testament prediction or from the life of Christ or from some New Testament subfulfilment (such as could be found in an earlier saint's life) with complete impunity. As Rosemund Tuve and others have pointed out, the interest of the typological allegorist was to

---

[35] A. C. Charity uses this term for the typological event which takes place between the moment of the Christ-example or Christ-pattern and its final and absolute fulfilment in the Second Coming. See *Events and their Afterlife*, 152-154, 160, 260.

demonstrate that certain essential truths were constantly recurring within human history. [36] Even if a writer borrowed and interchanged various motifs and metaphors, he would not in reality alter the essence of that basic verity which was his principal concern.

It is thus possible that the life of a saint, in which many borrowed motifs exist, can be understood even within the confines of ritual as mystic truth. We can accept Berceo's assertion that his story is true although we doubt that many things which he relates actually happened to Oria. [37] If they did not take place within the *exemplum* of her life, they had happened at another point within the typological tradition which her life illustrates. Berceo's *Vida de Santa Oria* thereby constitutes a valid subfulfilment of a typological pattern and it may be taken as a legitimate pole for typological comparison. We may view Oria as subfulfilling the Christ-pattern at several points in her life just as Facundus and Primitivus performed an acceptable *imitatio* with their deaths. [38]

I believe that the method used by those writers who composed in the manner of the «allegory of the theologians» is very similar to that employed by hagiographers. Just as the writer of saints' lives had to be working with at least a core of truth, so the author whose finished piece was acceptable for true typological comparison had to begin with a configuration of meaning naturally

[36] *Allegorical Imagery*, 405. Robert Burlin notices that «...what happened at one moment in time may be extended through all history... backward in the prefigurations of the Old Testament and forward in the spiritual experience of the Church and the individual believer» (*The Old English Advent: A Typological Commentary*, New Haven and London, 1968, 178), See Charity (160) for the same idea.

[37] Of course I admit that Berceo might have falsified various facts or exaggerated others for economic or political reason. See Brian Dutton, *La 'Vida de San Millán de la Cogolla', de Gonzalo de Berceo: estudio y edición crítica* (Colección Támesis. Serie A: Monografías 4; London, 1967), 175. However I do not feel that the Church in general, and as specific policy in the liturgy, could have accepted such actions, particularly in regard to that saint's life in Latin which was to be utilized within the office in ritual context. F. P. Pickering, *Literature and Art in the Middle Ages* (London, 1970), has pointed out that the iconography of the Crucifixion developed during the pre-Reformation period is «in the first place a Psalm illustration» (233). He believes that much of Christian art derived its images from the Old Testament prophecy of the New Testament event and not from the later happening itself. This is the point which I would also suggest in regard to literature.

[38] By the Christ-pattern I mean the trajectory of Jesus' life on earth which numerous New Testament texts such as John 13.36 hold up as an example for Christians. The individual cannot imitate the entirety of this pattern, but if the Christian attempts to follow Jesus his life should be assimilated consciously or unconsciously to that of the Saviour.

established in some manner in God's order. Beyond that basic outline the creative writer would be as free as the hagiographer to search the entirety of the typological tradition (and probably much else also) for referents with which to embellish and explain his work.

The question of the «allegory of the poets» and the «allegory of the theologians» may resolve itself into one of direction and orientation. The poet knows a «meaning» which he wishes to ornament with the language of symbolism. The theologian-author comes upon a series of events, grounded in historical or natural fact, within which he suspects there to be a reflection of God's divine order. He sets out to explain this sacramental significance, to interpret it for his fellow men and, finally, to cast it into literary form. The «allegory of the poets» is basically creative literature while the «allegory of the theologians» is akin in a way to expository writing in which the author has maintained a deep aesthetic interest. The theologian-writer does with a series of natural events what the expositors of the liturgy did: he explains hidden universals in things which he saw as naturally created phenomena. His basis for writing would be any sequence of events which he thought to be true whether something which he himself had witnessed or something which he had good authority to believe had happened. It might have been even a dream or vision since for the medieval such things were placed in the human mind by God. [39]

The works of Berceo illustrate the three possibilities open to the medieval writer interested in conveying doctrinal truths. In the body of the *Milagros* the poet has retold tales without allegorical embellishment which he undoubtedly believed to be true. In the Introduction to the *Milagros* he has conceived a completely allegorical setting which he wishes the reader to understand as a poetic fiction devised for aesthetic purposes. In the *Vida de Santa Oria* he has taken a story which he again must have seen as true and has posed it in a literary framework ornamented by symbolism.

---

[39] We can then accept the content of Oria's visions as true if we believe that she actually experienced them. I believe that the basis for the «reality» or «history» of the *Divine Comedy* must lie in a vision which Dante witnessed. It would provide foundation so that the poet could use the work as a typological pole. Doubtless the outline of this «truth» has been expanded a thousand times by the poet's great creative abilities.

It now becomes clear that the so-called «allegory of the theologians» can rightly be called «allegory» only by taking the term in its broadest sense. A better and more proper definition of the phenomenon is embellished or decorated history—if we understand history to mean a series of events which the writer looked upon as true. A very close connection does exist between this kind of writing and «poetic allegory» in that this artificial mode often is one of the embellishments used by the creative exegete to enrich his work.

The «allegory of the theologians» is by its very nature exegetical, implying the interpretation of a natural sign or action, while the «allegory of the poets» is an imaginatively created thing originating in the mind of the writer. To compose an «allegory of the theologians» an author would have to construct a literary creation upon or around an idea or set of ideas which he, at least, believed to be grounded in fact. Taken in its most narrow sense, a literary work conceived in terms of the «allegory of the theologians» would have to rest upon historical truth. But the very term «literature» implies some use of the creative imagination. Thus if a writer had a vision of reality which seemed to be totally at one with Christian doctrine, he might seek corroboration of his personal vision in some naturally occurring series of events. His own ideas would then coalesce with reality to form a basis for an aesthetically grounded work which could convey the essence of his vision to other men. He would be equally free to appropriate motifs from the typological tradition within which he was working. Robert Hollander has shown that in Canto II of the *Inferno* Dante simultaneously figures Adam looking up to the place from which he fell, Noah surviving the flood and Aeneas setting out into the Libyan desert as well. When Dante begins to move along the *piaggia deserta*, he suggests Noah, Aeneas, and even the Children of Israel after crossing the Red Sea. [40] Obviously this «allegory of the theologians» would in many respects very closely resemble the «allegory of the poets». The distinguishing factor would be whether the poet or writer emphasized his own «responsibility» [41] in the invention of the

---

[40] See Hollander, 260.

[41] If the writer did not emphasize his own responsibility, then he was implying that his material had the stamp of God's authority upon it. Hugh of St. Victor seems to sense something of this when he states that the entire world «...quasi quidam liber est, scriptus digito Dei, hoc est virtute divina creatus, et singulae crea-

allegorical framework. If he did, then we can only conclude that he saw his allegory as an artistic way of demonstrating his ideas and nothing more. If he attempted to claim historical validity for his framework, he was placing the responsibility for the veracity of the facts of the case not upon himself but upon God who is the author of all natural occurrences. He, the creative exegete, only explained the facts and conveyed them to the reader in an attractive manner.

Seen in this light any literary work composed according to the «allegory of the theologians» would be a kind of artistic gloss added to or built around a core of natural truth which the writer had found expressed in one way or the other. The effect of his artistic «glossing» would have been to make the semblance of the divine order present in the source more discernible and more aesthetically interesting to the alert reader. [42]

Leo Spitzer seems to suggest this *modus operandi* when he discusses Marie de France's prologue to her *Lais* «... in any poetic work there is only one doctrine, the «right» («Paiens unt tort, Chrestiens unt *dreit*»). Marie knows that her poetic tales have a Christian significance and that the subtlety of future commentators will be exercised to discover that immutable Christian truth...» [43] If Spitzer were right, then Marie could not have viewed her fables as «allegory of the poets» because she herself

---

turae quasi figurae quaedam sunt non humano placito inventae, sed divine arbitrio institutae ad manifestandum invisibilium Dei sapientiam» (*PL*, 176, 814. cited and trans. Robert Jordan, *Chaucer and the Shape of Creation*, Cambridge, Mass., 1967, 28). If a figure were invented by human will *(placito)*, it would not be valid except as an artificial explanation. The Moslem attitude on this point is interesting in that it is very strong in its warning to the artist who would invent by his own will. «The artist as a shaper of forms is felt to be in rivalry with the Lord. On Judgment Day the makers of figures will be asked to inhale life into their works; but they will fail and be consigned to eternal punishment» (Gustave von Grunebaum, «The Aesthetic Foundation of Arabic Literature», *CL*, 4, 1952, 334).

[42] Robert Jordan sees the medieval writer as artistically «constructing» his work from source material. He quotes Alain of Lille (*De planctu naturae, PL*, 210, 451): «Poets combine historical events with fictional entertainments to form an elegant structure, so that from a suitable joining together of the narrative itself a more elegant picture may result...» and then goes on to explain «In this view the art of poetry is primarily a manipulative art, consisting in the conscious, deliberate disposition of clearly delimited parts. Art so conceived is properly regarded as 'structure' rather than 'expression'» (34). Jordan believes that Dante followed the same line of reasoning in his work: «Dante regards a poetic fiction as a material substance which can be deliberately «woven» then draped over the truth, and, at will and with the requisite cunning, removed... Plainly Dante understood literary art to be a process of construction, in the most literal and unsubtle sense of the term» (35-37).

[43] «The Prologue to the *Lais* of Marie de France and Medieval Poetics», *MP*, 41 (1943-44), 100-101.

would have known what meaning she had meant to put there. On the other hand if she took pagan fables as naturally occurring phenomena in which she saw the outline of Christian doctrine, and rewrote them so as to make the form of the fables more artistically pleasing, she would be composing «an allegory of the theologians». [44] She could expect future commentators to find more and more substance of Christian truth in the source which she herself had first pointed out. They could also help to make this substance clearer and more attractive. The «topic of humility» which writers used to ask future readers to change the work, if they were able, in order to better it, would be elementary to the whole purpose of writing such an allegory. A medieval writer who wrote to glorify God by explaining His design in historical or natural events was not, in any sense, pouring out his own feelings as important in themselves. He was attempting to make clear the divine plan by which the universe was governed. Anyone who could take his work a step further as a demonstration of truth was compelled to do so. If the writer bonded his exegesis directly to what he was explaining without artistically weaving thesis and interpretation together, he would be composing a straightforward expository work. But when he only alludes to his exegesis, and when his explanation is aesthetically bound to the substance, the writer creates artistic possibilities which project his piece into the realm of literature.

Montalvo in his prologue to his 16th century rendition of the *Amadís* asks the reader to compare the battles described in the work to those which he has personally witnessed. The majority, the author admits, may not conform to truth—but what of the others? «... ¿Qué tomaremos de las unas y otras, que algún fruto provechoso nos acarreen? Por cierto, a mi ver, otra cosa no salvo los buenos enxemplos y doctrinas, que más a la salvación nuestra se allegaren, porque seyendo permitido de ser imprimida en nuestros coraçones la gracia del muy alto Señor para a ellas nos llegar, tomemos por alas con que nuestras

---

[44] Américo Castro points out that epic material was often looked upon as being as full of truth as the chronicles: «for a historian as learned as Alphonse X, the *cantares de gesta* were as believable as the chronicles of Rodrigo Jiménez de Rada. If there was no dividing wall between poetry and reality for the minstrel-poets, neither did the historians distinguish between poetic legend and verified history» (*The Structure of Spanish History*, trans. Edmund L. King, Princeton, 1954, 296).

ánimas suban a la alteza de la gloria para donde fueron criadas». [45]
What Montalvo is saying is that the grace of God will aid us in
seeing these battles as illustrative of Christian truths. He is
thus inviting the reader to interpret the events of the *Amadís*
in the light of Christian experience. Only a few lines further
along Montalvo says that he has aided the reader's search by
adding certain *emiendas* to the work.

> ... en los quales cinco libros como quiera que hasta aquí más por
> patrañas que por crónicas eran tenidos, son con las tales emiendas
> acompañados de tales enxemplos y doctrinas, que con justa causa se
> podrán comparar a los livianos y febles saleros de corcho, que con
> tiras de oro y de plata son encarcelados y guarnescidos... (9)

If the books of the *Amadís* had been taken for history, they
would have been suitable for study as illustrative of God's divine
plan. As *patrañas* they can be seen as no more than puny inventions of the mind of man. Montalvo claims to perceive more in
these books (and thereby implies their historical validity). By
adding the *emiendas* he clarifies and delineates the Christian truths
which he finds there. The comparison of the emended story
to a cork saltshaker, worthless in itself but valuable because of
its gold and silver adornments, gives us a perfect understanding
of Montalvo's point. The story of *Amadís* is valueless without
the outline of Christian meaning which it shadows. His *emiendas*
bring that outline into relief. [46] This would suggest that
Montalvo was aware of a tradition in which a writer revitalized
(or claimed to) source material in which he perceived the essence
of doctrinal teachings. Whether Montalvo himself was serious
in his exhortation or whether he was merely using a shopworn
topos to justify purely imaginative writings, is of no consequence. [47]

[45] Rodríguez de Montalvo, *Amadís de Gaula,* ed. Edwin B. Place, I (Madrid,
1959), 9.
[46] Deneef sees the same process in *The Faerie Queen:* «...we can see that
Spenser is, in many instances, imposing an allegorical structure on *The Faerie Queen,*
we cannot see this in medieval poetry, for there was no need to impose an allegorical
structure. Mere mention of a phrase, a word, an action, a figure on the surface
of a poem would suggest patterns of meaning which the audience brought to the
work themselves» («Robertson and the Critics», 217). Of course I would disagree
in that I suspect that the earlier writer was «imposing» an outline to signal the
inherent meaning in much the same manner as Spenser save that his method was not
so obvious and he expected his reader to make the transference from one plane to
another more readily than did Spenser.
[47] Place believes that the *Amadís* was written with at least three definite
objectives in mind: «1) pintar un caballero perfecto a lo artúrico en lucha con los

The idea would have to have been alive at one time in order to have produced an imitable tradition. [48]

An interesting problem arises in a literary work when the surface plane suggests another level of meaning.

> What kinds of relationship are possible between the literal level and the extra-literal meanings in literary allegory... and secondly, to what extent does this «allegory» produce a continuous level of meaning beyond the literal, and to what extent merely a number of separate illusions? [49]

To some degree Singleton has answered this question, at least in regard to the «allegory of the poets» when he says that in a work written according to this method the literal plane must yield «another *true* meaning or it has no excuse for being». [50] In Berceo's *Introduction* to the *Milagros* one can see that this interpretation is correct. The entire line of meaning on the surface plane—the traveler's arrival in the *locus amoenus* and his adventures

males de su época; 2) alabar la proeza de los caballeros; 3) de más importancia para el autor—demostrar que en el «mezclamiento de los malos consejeros consiste el mayor peligro al trono y al bienestar del país» (*Amadís de Gaula,* III, 931). Of course Montalvo could have demonstrated all these points by means of the literal plane of the story without recourse to allegory. It remains to be demonstrated whether the primary plane has a set of spiritual referents. The effect of typology would be to make those worthy deeds accomplished by Amadís reflect others realized by that most perfect of knights—Jesus Christ.

[48] Gonzalo de Berceo makes an interesting comparison in the Introduction to the *Milagros* when, in speaking of the composition of the four Gospels, he says that the Virgin «emended» what the evangelists wrote. «Quanto escrivien ellos, ella lo emendava» (22). The implication seems to be that, more than correcting the grammar and punctuation, the Virgin was filling the Gospels with divine «truth». This idea of emending a text to show the outline of Christian truth (or in the case of the Virgin actually placing the truth there) seems to be related to the «versos extraños» metaphor in the *Libro de buen amor* (1634). Spitzer queries whether these «strange verses» could not be myths «that are pagan and mysterious—needing allegorical interpretation» («The Prologue to the *Lais* of Marie de France...», 41, n. 5). The same metaphor, found in the *Divine Comedy* (Inf. X, 61), occurs in slightly different form in a short poem *El auctor al lector* at the end of the prologue to the *Palmerín:* «Aquí Palmerín os es descubierto, los hechos mostrando de su forta-leza; / leedle, pues es historia de alteza, / en todo apacible con dulce concier-to; / coged con sentido en ello despierto / todas las flores de dichos notables, / oyen-do sentencias que son saludables, / robando la fruta de ajenos güertos...» (*Libros de caballerías,* ed. A. Bonilla y San Martín, II, NBAE, 11, Madrid, 1908, 4). The author in asking the reader to catch with *sentido despierto* the *sentencias* taken from stolen fruit of *ajenos güertos* is clearly alluding to a significance beyond the surface layer, and he is not himself assuming the responsibility for having placed this stratum within the work. With his «strange gardens» metaphor he can imply not only a sense of mystery but also that the fruit of these gardens was filled with some sort of natural truth.

[49] «Chaucer and Medieval Allegory», *ELH,* 30 (1963), 192.

[50] «Dante's Allegory», 81.

there—has, save for the grammatical framework itself, another significance which Berceo interprets for the reader. He does not pretend that we should value the adventure for itself.

In a work composed according to the «allegory of the theologians» quite another approach is taken. Let us suppose that a medieval poet or writer decides to embellish some series of natural or historical events in which he perceives the outline of important truths. This series of events might be a saint's life, a pious legend, a vision which he or someone else had experienced or even an adventure tale grounded in antiquity which seemed to possess around it the aura of historical truth. The author rewrites and refurbishes the whole so that the significance which he sees there becomes more apparent, more fascinating, and more aesthetically appealing to future readers. If he is successful and if he is a true artist, the product of his labor will possess the authenticity of the source translated into a new and vital artistic form. The finished product presents the critic with two distinct panoramas which he must attempt to see as a whole. The first is the fabric of the source which is the foundation for the literal plane of the story. The second is the level of meaning, perhaps continuous, perhaps fragmentary, which the author's *emiendas*, his creative innovations, have caused to stand out in relief above the literal level of the source story.

A medieval work, conceived in the manner of the «allegory of the theologians» could be then two *exempla* in one since the literal level as well as the referents which derive from it might present the reader with truth. The primary and secondary planes would move together in a fashion similar to musical counterpoint, except that at times the spiritual line would not be present. Sometimes the two would complement one another's meanings perfectly just as the various parts in a Bach concerto support one another. In other places the two could move in a diametrically opposed manner, the literal level suggesting one thing or one viewpoint while its complementary plane implied a meaning completely contradictory to that on the surface. The important point is that the meaning implied on the literal level, which Stephen Langton in his sermons referred to as *moralitas secundum litteram* [51] could often be just as important as that on

[51] Beryl Smalley, *The Study of the Bible in the Middle Ages* (2nd ed., New York, 1952), 190.

the secondary level. Thus when Zifar saves the widowed ruler of Galapia from her enemies, we must value his actions as an example of the chivalric injunction to aid widows and orphans. At the same time the episode might suggest some truth from sacred history or the life of Christ which would be the secondary meaning.

Medieval man looked upon the Christ-experience (particularly the Incarnation) as the fulcrum upon which all history was balanced. Everything that had occurred before the advent of Jesus pointed in some mystical way to His earthly mission. Once the Christ-experience had happened within linear time, those who saw this as central to history could not help but adopt a view which was Janus-faced. They gazed back in wonder upon the Incarnation, death, and Resurrection of Jesus while simultaneously looking forward to the Second Coming which was to be the absolute fulfilment of Old Testament, New Testament and the present. The events of Christ's life, and the significance growing out of these events, would eventually come to complete fulfilment in the Second Coming and the establishment of the celestial kingdom. The medieval Christian believed that, in this intervening time between Christ and the Second Coming, he and others were participating in some strange mystical way both in the wonderful experiences of Jesus' life on earth and in the joyous existence of the heavenly city. [52] Until the moment of fulfilment the essence of Christ's example would find echo in the lives of individual Christians. Just as the Christ-pattern was reflected backward and could be glimpsed in Old Testament events, so obviously it would also be seen in New Testament time.

The role of the knight is in many respects analogous to that of the saint and is, in fact, more apropos as an *imitatio Christi* for the active life. Contemplation and the ascetic way had their

[52] Charity, 160. Morton Bloomfield points out that the Middle Ages tended to place overwhelming emphasis on a few events out of history. «These events were often assimilated to an extra-historical reality. Christ is sacrificed every minute of the day, and man continually falls, as he did once in the long, long ago. Every Enactment of the Mass goes through the redemptive process all over again» («Chaucer's Sense of History», *JEGP*, 51 (1952), 302). It was, of course, the meanings of these historical events which the artist-exegete hoped to find recurring in source material which he could then take and recast, rebuild, restructure, emend or weave into a new and more aesthetically appealing literary form. Bloomfield does not specifically suggest that the Second Coming of Christ also has a bearing upon intermediate events, but certainly his reasoning would in addition suggest this.

place but the strong arm of the «caballero» was needed if the Faith was to be preserved and the weak and helpless defended. [53] Doubtless the real deeds of a *miles christi* who existed would have been viewed as worthy for typological comparison with the Christ-pattern. God could demonstrate his plan in history through the actions of those who fought His holy wars as readily as in the lives of those who dedicated themselves to sanctity. In the *Zifar* the knight's quest may be seen as a divinely inspired mission when the old and feeble King of Mentón recognizes Zifar as a saviour sent by the Almighty to protect the land from its enemies. «... cuydo que sea cavallero de Dios, que nos ha aqui enbiado para nos defender e lidiar por nos.» [54] It is my thesis that the story of Zifar, which the author wished us to see as true history, stands as one typological pole, a New Testament era subfulfilment, of a divine pattern visible again and again throughout time.

[53] See Lull, *Libre de cavalleria*, I, 212-213.
[54] *El libro del Cavallero Zifar*, ed. Charles P. Wagner (Ann Arbor, 1929), 153. All further citations from the *Zifar* will be taken from this edition. Spitzer has suggested that the hero's life has a transcendental meaning which, properly understood, makes it susceptible to typological explanation: «From every hero, as from every saint, there emanates a legendary tradition, a «gloss» superadded to the original text of his life. Every exemplary life is a Bible—and who says Bible says exegesis; cf. the epithet dedicated by the Marquis de Santillana to the Virgin of Guadalupe: *texto e admirabil glosa...*» (MP, 41, 97, n. 1).

CHAPTER THREE

THE *ZIFAR*, STRUCTURE AND MEANING

It is likely that the structure of the *Zifar* is based upon that of the medieval university sermon. [1] In the Middle Ages two sermon forms were common. One is a simple point-by-point commentary upon a chapter from Scripture. The other, which probably originated in the university communities, had a complicated organization which derived from the rules of the Classical oration. This «university sermon» opened with a theme, generally a verse from the Bible, and continued into a protheme or exordium. Here the preacher wished to demonstrate the importance of the theme for his listeners and thereby interest them in his message. After the protheme came a short prayer where the speaker invoked God's blessing upon himself, the congregation and upon all things. He would then repeat the theme for the benefit of latecomers and also to remind his listeners of its importance.

After this the preacher would begin the «introduction of the theme». Here he would make a transition from the theme and protheme to the body or *dilatio* of the sermon. Since this *dilatio* was normally expanded from three important points drawn from the theme, it was necessary for him to present these points and to explain how he would develop them. Various methods are suggested in the *artes praedicandi* to aid the preacher in joining his theme and *dilatio*. [2]

---

[1] See my «The *Libro del Cavallero Zifar* and the Medieval University Sermon», Viator, I (1970), 207-221.

[2] See C. S. Baldwin, *Ancient Rhetoric and Poetic* (reprint, Gloucester, Mass., 1959), 35, for a discussion of the oratorical devices *narratio-argumentatio* which the author of the *Zifar* seems to have used.

39

In the prologue after the author of the *Zifar* has finished the story of the translation of the body of the Cardinal from Rome to Toledo, he ponders the meaning of the episode and concludes that Ferrand Martines performed this great deed because he owed so much to the Cardinal.

> E çiertas sy costa grande fizo el Arçidiano en este camino, mucho le es de gradesçer porque lo enpleo muy bien, reconosçiendo la merçed que del Cardenal resçebiera e la criança que en el feziera, asy commo lo deven fazer todos los omes de buen entendimiento e de buen conosçer e que bien e merçed resçiben de otro. Onde bien aventurado fue el señor que se trabajo de fazer buenos criados e leales; ca estos atales nin les fallesçeran en la vida nin despues; ca lealtad les faze acordarse del bienfecho que resçebieron en vida e en muerte. (6)

Ferrand Martines probably had received his appointment as Archdeacon of Madrid from Cardinal Gonzalo when he was Archbishop of Toledo and would, thus, have been very beholden to him. The author of the *Zifar* begins with this historical episode because he wishes to extract his theme from it. He wants to emphasize that all men granted *buen entendimiento* and *buen conosçer* should, like Ferrand Martines, repay *bien e merçed* which they receive from another. This principle, of great importance for medieval man, can be summarized in the Latin dictum *redde quod debes* which means that every man must repay what he owes—to God as well as to his fellow man.

Redde quod debes, although not a biblical verse, renders very well the meaning of the parable of the good and bad servants in Matthew 25. For the Middle Ages this parable meant that the Christian was obliged to use well and increase the «talents» entrusted to him or risk damnation. Obviously the parable would be particularly applicable to the life of a Christian knight whose duty was to serve God by doing good and protecting the helpless. For example Matthew 25 is used in the Old French *Queste del saint graal* where a hermit warns Lancelot that he must begin to employ his God-given talents for the good of man.

> ... «Sire, fet Lancelot, ceste semblance que vos m'avez ci mostree, de ces trois serjanz qui avoient receuz les besanz, me desconforte assez plus que nule autre chose. Car je sai bien que Jhesucrist me garni en m'enfance de toutes les bones graces que onques nus

hons poïst avoit; et por ce qu'il me fu si larges de prest et je li ai
si mal rendu ce qu'il m'ot baillié... [3]

From this day forward the knight will attempt to devote himself
to serving God. The author of the *Zifar*, instead of using
Jesus' parable in Matthew 25 as an illustration, has chosen the
story of the translation of the body of Cardinal Gonzalo. But
the significance of both *exempla* is the same—the good servant
will repay what he owes to his master. «Onde bien aventurado
fue el señor que se trabajo de fazer buenos criados e leales.»

If *redde quod debes* is the sermonic theme of the *Zifar*, then
everything that Zifar and Roboán accomplished would have to be
understood as a fulfilment of this principle, either to God or to
their fellow man. The three divisions of the *Zifar*, the «Cavallero de Dios y rey de Mentón», the «Castigos del rey de Mentón»,
and the «Hechos de Roboán» would be homiletic *exempla* used
in the manner of the university sermon to clarify and explain the
message implied in the main theme and subsidiary themes
deriving from it. The method used by the author to construct
his *exempla* would be that of typological or figural allegory set
for strength and effect against the cyclically recurring liturgical
seasons.

In the previous chapter I have hoped to explain the difference
between the two medieval concepts of the «allegory of the poets»
and the figural «allegory of the theologians». It is necessary to
discuss the problem of *figura* because the author of the *Zifar* in
that place in the work which corresponds to the *argumentatio*
of a university sermon implies that in order to receive full benefit
from it his reader must interpret the work as also having a spiritual force. Readers would have been willing to look to the
Zifar (or to the tale which was its prototype) for moral example
had they believed it to be history, since God places meaning in
true events which are written by Him. But it was possible
that they might doubt the veracity of its happenings, and since
the author could not prove that these actions really took place,
he feared that his reader might doubt the value of the book.

E porque este libro nunca aparesçio escripto en este lenguaje fasta
agora, nin lo vieron los omes nin lo oyeron, cuydaron algunos que

[3] *La Queste del Saint Graal,* ed. Albert Pauphilet (Les Classiques Français du
Moyen Age, Paris, 1923), 64.

non fueran verdaderas las cosas que se y contienen, nin ay provecho
en ellas, non parando mentes al entendimiento de las palabras nin
queriendo curar en ellas. (9)

To avoid these suspicions the author points out that valuable
examples can be gleaned from the *Zifar* even if the work is not
grounded in truth.

Pero commoquier que verdaderas non fuesen, non las deven tener
en poco nin dubdar en ellas fasta que las oyan todas conplidamente
e vean el entendimiento dellas, e saquen ende aquello que entendie-
ren de que se pueden aprovechar; ca de cada cosa que es y dicha
pueden tomar buen enxienplo e buen consejo para saber traer su
vida mas çierta e mas segura, sy bien quisieren usar dellas; (9-10)

Previously in his prologue the author of the *Zifar* claimed that
he was reworking a story originally written in *caldeo* and subsequently translated into Latin and then into Romance. (6)   The
implication here is that even if the events of this story were not
true, the «message» implied in them would be valid because «de
cada cosa que es y dicha pueden tomar buen enxiemplo».   The
author seems to be suggesting something of the idea held by
the Victorines and others that all created things (including written
phenomena) reflect the invisible creation of God. [4]   But this is
not the case, for immediately afterwards he gives the well-known
nucleus-cortex image via the metaphor of a nut (que ha de parte
de fuera fuste seco e tiene el fruto ascondido dentro) and then
proceeds to what is basically a definition of the «allegory of the
poets».   He says that the «sabios antiguos» wrote useful books
in which they placed *exempla* using the metaphor of birds and
animals.   There was no meaning in the forms themselves (en
que non ay entendimiento nin razon nin sentido ninguno),
however they could be interpreted «en manera de fablillas, que
dieron entendimiento de buenos enxiemplos e de buenos castigos,
e fezieronnos entender e creer lo que non aviemos visto nin
creyemos que podria esto ser verdat...» (10).   Just as the ancients
made things clearer by means of «fablillas», «... asy... los padres
santos fezieron a cada uno de los siervos de Iesu Cristo ver commo
por espejo e sentir verdaderamente e creer de todo en todo que
son verdaderas las palabras de la fe de Iesu Cristo, e maguer el

---

[4]   See Chydenius, *Theory of Medieval Symbolism,* 10.

fecho non vieron; por que ninguno non deve dudar en las cosas nin las menospreçiar, fasta que vean lo que quieren dezir e commo se deven entender».

At the beginning of the Christian era Philo and later the School of Alexandria had discarded to a large degree the literal meaning of Scripture and had concentrated upon the spiritual significances conveyed by the surface plane. The School of Antioch and the early Latin fathers reasserted the importance of the literal and followed St. Paul's example in conceiving a Christian allegory in which the event on the literal surface was viewed as true yet recalling or foreshadowing another event or meaning which would be equally valid. [5] Although the Pauline viewpoint was to predominate, in the later Middle Ages the conflict continued concerning whether biblical events were «true» in themselves or whether they were merely metaphors used to convey truths. Chydenius points out that the neoplatonic Christian view which held that all created things are symbols, that is that they were in some way demonstrative of the meaning of God's universe, was not accepted by all schoolmen in the 12th and 13th centuries. [6] William of Auvergne for example did not believe that events in the Bible had a significance in themselves but felt that it was the expositor who used the circumstances of the event in order to explain and make clear some difficult facet of Christian thought. [7]

Now this seems precisely to be the line of reasoning which the author of the *Zifar* is describing in his *argumentatio*. The implication is not that the «padres santos» were finding real meanings in the Scriptures, but that they were using events in the Bible in the manner of «fablillas» to explain difficult facts of the Christian faith. Applied to the *Zifar*, this would suggest, as the author states, that the whole literal plane of the story is no more than «fuste seco», a worthless hull to be discarded after it had been translated into a meaning on the allegorical plane. The literal level would have no reason to exist other than to furnish the vehicle for conveying the significance of the secondary stratum and further, as I have pointed out in regard to the Introduction to Berceo's *Milagros*, every event on the real plane

[5] See Chydenius, *Typological Problem in Dante*, 25-30.
[6] Chydenius, *Theory*, 20-22.
[7] *Ibid.*, 22.

would have to allude to some meaning on the allegorical level.
This clearly cannot be the case with the *Zifar*. The reader
feels that he is following a «real» story of a real knight and his
family. There is no indication that the work is artificial or
simply contrived, as in the case of the Introduction to the *Milagros*, in order to lay the groundwork for a point-by-point correspondence. Undoubtedly certain things in the *Zifar* (such as
the names of persons and places) do have meanings which allude
to something beyond the concrete significance of the object
itself. But there is by no means a continuous layer of correspondence by which every event and phenomenon on the surface
plane of the story can be directly referred to a spiritual idea on
a secondary stratum.

The solution to this problem probably lies in the rules of
a literary genre which we do not completely understand. Jean
Leclercq points out that in defiance of Isidore's separation of
narrative into two types—the *historia* and *fabula*—, one finds
often in the Middle Ages historical material juxtaposed with
imaginary or legendary material.[8] Medieval men remained
aware of the distinction between historical fact and creative
fiction but in order to exhort or edify, they freely mixed the two
without giving any indication that they were passing from a true
statement to a dubious one. This method is particularly
characteristic of the *Vitae sanctorum* where, Leclercq warns us,
we must expect to learn not historical verities but «their ideas on
monastic life and on sanctity as illustrated in non-historical
themes» (206). The medieval neoplatonic worldview was interested in universal and eternal ideas, not the transitory events
of history. If the modern critic is able to adopt the outlook
of the Middle Ages, then he can appreciate that legend, if it
serves to illustrate the point better than history, becomes in
effect «truer than history» (206).

This certainly is the view of the author of the *Zifar*. He
contends that the story of his hero is true (18). It is one, however,
which occurred in another time and in another place. Further
he has embellished this story with certain «emiendas» which,
while making the meaning clearer, also, because of their artifi-
ciality, add an element of doubt. By insisting that the reader

[8] Leclercq, *The Love of Learning*, 205.

bear in mind the idea that «de cada cosa que es y dicha pueden tomar buen enxiemplo...» he is able to avoid the question «... pero commoquier que verdaderas non fuesen...» One might say that he begs the question by reminding his reader that the general purpose of the work is edification; thus the combination of materials which compose the book, both true and fictive, must be appreciated principally with that end in mind.

The method of allegory used in the *Zifar* which I shall attempt to explain bears little resemblance to the «fablillas» constructed by the ancients to expound doctrine. Far from being «fuste seco» the literal level of the work is as charged with meaning as the secondary plane. Certainly the numerous virtuous actions which Zifar and his son Roboán perform must be seen as powerful illustrations of what the author of the work considered to be the proper course of action for a Christian knight. One can readily see that the *Zifar* is an active example of those precepts offered by such a work as Lull's *Libre del ordre de cavalleria.* The principal explanation as to why the author does not overly emphasize the importance of the surface stratum is probably his desire to make sure that all of his readers should be aware of and search for the symbolic meaning of the work. [9] Second, the author could not prove that the events in the book really happened and therefore their veracity might have been doubted by the suspicious reader. Since only real events, ordained by the hand of God, were generally accepted as having true spiritual significance, then ones conceived and fostered by the human mind might well be suspect. The author manages to avoid confronting this problem while at the same time using that figural method which was reserved for the explication of true historical happenings.

The «sabios antiguos» composed fables as vehicles for demonstrating truths; the author of the *Zifar* found a work which he believed to be basically historical. Within the structure of the piece he saw the outline of certain Christian truths. The work is old and hallowed by time. He is sure that the story is true and that the hero's life has significance which can be of use to man, so he imposes upon the text as he found it certain «emiendas» (6) [10] which give better artistic form to the configuration of

---

[9] Medieval writers commonly claimed that readers should have to search for the meaning in a piece in order properly to appreciate it. See Chapter One, n. 7 for reference to such a place in the writings of Juan Manuel.

[10] See Chapter Two, n. 48.

Christian truth which he sees there. By means of these «emiendas» the author extracts for the reader a spiritual level which he finds shadowed by the surface plane of the work. He is, by placing a superstructure upon the story which makes this stratum stand out, performing a work of exegesis—that is, he clarifies for the reader what the story means by signaling its interior significance. [11] He is imposing an outline which would suggest to the alert or «subtle» reader that the text was demonstrating old truths in new and informative ways. The reader, by following the line of thought skillfully conceived and artistically woven into the text by the author, could profit by gaining new understanding and insight into problems previously difficult or unclear.

Of course the modern reader or interpreter of a medieval work is ever in danger of falling into what John Halverson refers to as «template criticism», the superimposition of the modern critic's own preconceived pattern upon the text which then allows only a certain design of meaning to appear. [12] Certainly anyone who has ever consulted the indices of allegorical figures in the *Patrologia latina* is aware that a critic, by carefully choosing among the varied and often conflicting interpretations given, might be able to establish any number of meanings for a text depending upon how he arranged and contrasted his symbols. But this would only be possible if the author of the work in question had not given the reader any sort of textual indication which would direct him toward the correct analysis. In the *Zifar* the author

[11] In effect, the author of the *Zifar* follows a procedure very similar to the one described by A. C. Charity which produced the artistic treatments of the life of St. Francis. Charity says that the real events of the saint's life, the true history, becomes stylized to a certain extent, because of didactic and aesthetic considerations, but not completely so: «The saint's life demands a special kind of treatment in order to interpret its effect, and not just mirror its action and its chronology. And it is specially interesting in our context that one of the features of St. Francis' life which produced such 'stylization' from the earliest 'lives' of the saint increasingly down to the work of Fra Bartolomeo of Pisa at the end of the Fourteenth century, was that which the title of Fra Bartolomeo's work precisely expresses; *De Conformitate Vitae B. Francisci ad Vitam Domini Jesu.* In this latter work —as also in paintings of up to seventy years earlier— the fundamentally theological point in the imitatio Christi is brought out by setting event opposite event from the life of Saviour and servant» (254). What Charity is of course suggesting is that the medieval Christian artist, when confronted with an example of such virtue as that of St. Francis, could not help but assimilate the life of the saint, in one way or the other, to that of the supreme exemplar, Jesus Christ. In the next chapter I hope to demonstrate that the author, by means of his *emiendas,* has converted the adventures of the knight and his family into an *imitatio Christi.*

[12] «Template Criticism: *Sir Gawain and the Green Knight*», MP, 67 (1969-70), 138.

does offer such textual aids as a help to the reader in searching for the «kernel of meaning». If the critic interprets details within the context outlined by the author, he may well make mistakes but his errors can only be within the range of possibility which the outline demarks.

The author of the *Zifar* has imposed his *emiendas*, that is he has made to stand out in relief certain verities suggested to him by his source text, in two ways. First he gave names to persons, places and things in the work which allegorically describe their function within his framework of meaning. [13] By calling the chief character in the book «Zifar», which resembles the Arabic word for traveler, the author placed upon him the whole range of connotation associated with the concept of *homo viator* in the Middle Ages. [14] Zifar's older son bears the name Garfín, little prince in Arabic, which denotes his position as heir apparent to his father in the kingdom of Mentón. Grima is a corrupt form of Arabic *karima* which means generous or virtuous, qualities certainly fitting the noble wife of Zifar. Names in the *Zifar* are signposts which aid the reader in perceiving the outline of meaning sensed in the work by the author.

The second way by means of which the author of the work aided his reader in following the line of suggestion inherent in the romance was to set the actions of the book, performed by characters with symbolic titles in places with meaningful names, against a background of the liturgical seasons. By skillful allusion to the circumstances of the event being commemorated or recalled in the liturgy, he is able to identify his character in time and space with the biblical figure or event which was the reason for the celebration. [15]

[13] See James Burke, «Names and the Significance of Etymology in the *Libro del Cavallero Cifar*», *RR,* 59 (1968), 161-173.

[14] See Gerhart B. Ladner, «Homo Viator: Mediaeval Ideas on Alienation and Order», *Spec.,* 42 (1967), 233-259.

[15] This same tradition seems to have been still active three hundred years later in the Golden Age drama. Alan Soons points out that the liturgical date is often used in Lope's plays to underline the meaning in Christian terms. In *Peribáñez* the dramatist establishes concord between the subject matter of the play and the doctrine of the Feast of the Assumption («Towards an Interpretation of *El Caballero de Olmedo*», *RF,* 73, 1961, 165). Soons sees *El Caballero de Olmedo,* I think, in essentially the same way that I view the *Zifar.* «*El Caballero de Olmedo* is not... an allegory... Rather it illustrates exceptionally well what the historical or legendary bases of his plays signified for Lope: opportunities for demonstrating poetically how there is an endless oscillation of type between such a basis and some symbolic act conceived as being outside time» (168).

Grima is saved by the intervention of the Virgin from a group of evil merchants who abduct her from Zifar. It becomes clear that the author has conceived the entire episode which treats her abduction and subsequent rescue by Mary as a kind of paean of praise to the Mother of God, illustrative of a number of commonplaces of the marian miracle tales. [16] Grima reaches the port of Galán (recuperation in Arabic) on the day of the Assumption, the most important of the feasts dedicated to Mary. After nine years of sojourn in the land of Orbín (widowed or orphaned in Latin), Zifar's wife is seen as a figure for the Virgin in that she is a kind of «New Eve» purified by her trials. She is ready to take her place beside her husband, now the king of Mentón, who in the Easter and Pentecost seasons had himself put off the «old man» in sin and had become associated with the «new man» in Christ.

The meaning of names and the associations of the liturgical season aid the author of the *Zifar* in assimilating the meaning of his work to the mainstream of Christian experience. The happenings of the book take on significances which are evocative of past events in Christian history or suggestive of ones prophesied as yet to come. Grima is a «New Eve». Zifar in his journey to become king of Mentón is following an intricate pattern which can be seen to recapitulate certain aspects of the life of Christ. These personages and events in the *Zifar* which recall things from the Bible demonstrate that certain essential truths of Christian history, whether past or yet to come, are constantly shadowed within the realm of human life and experience. [17] There is never an exact correspondence between some action of Zifar's and one of Christ's recorded in the Gospels because it is the «meaning» implied in the example given by Jesus and not the precise circumstance which is important for the Christian. The author hopes to suggest to his reader that this meaning is constantly recurring in the lives of all Christians who attempt to keep their lives in harmony with Christ's example.

Because the purpose of the author was to set up a series of figural correspondences between persons and events in the

---

[16] See James Burke, «Symbolic Allegory in the Portus Salutaris Episode in the *Libro del Cavallero Cifar*», *KRQ*, 15 (1968), 68-84.

[17] Robertson refers to the «continuous present» where eternal realities touch and influence what happens within linear time as an essential part of the allegorical situation (*Preface to Chaucer*, 301).

Zifar and others out of Christian history, his *modus operandi* is very close to being that of the «allegory of the theologians». He has seen God's truth in his source material and has made it stand out principally by the meanings of names and by reference to the liturgical seasons. He insists that his reader view his source material, if not strictly as historical, then as illustrative of divine truth in the same way as history.

Besides imposing *emiendas* to bring into relief the essences of meaning inherent in the source material, the author of the *Zifar* has in two places woven into his work adventure segments which clearly seem to be «allegories of the poet» in that the occurrences described within them do not harmonize with the mood of reality which pervades most of the book. Miraculous events do happen in the *Zifar*, such as the resurrection of the Señora de Galapia (66-67) or the salvation of Grima by the Virgin, but these marvels are completely in line with orthodox Catholic thinking in regard to the supernatural. On the other hand the incidents which befall el Cavallero Atrevido in the Lady of the Lake episode in the first *exemplum* (226-242) and the strange experiences of Roboán in the third have a mystery about them which seems to derive more from the art of Satan than that of Christ.

I believe that the *Islas Dotadas* episode, where Roboán travels to the abode of Fortune, is an elaborate allegory designed to illustrate the adverse effects of unbridled *cupiditas* upon a young and unsuspecting ruler. [18] Whereas the reader could accept most of the experiences of Roboán as historical, the *Islas Dotadas* episode, with its strange boat which unaided bears the young prince across the sea to a mysterious island where enchanted maidens await him, is clearly beyond the context of reality. The small vessel is not a real boat but a representation of the mild *curiositas* which caused the young knight to risk exile by asking the Emperor of Triguida the forbidden question concerning why he never laughed. The kingdom of Nobleza is the realm of Fortune where man must depend upon the turns of Chance's wheel for his destiny. The horse which tears Roboán away from Nobleza is a figure for the *codicia* which would not allow him to remain content with his lot. One can, in short, explain

---

[18] See James Burke, «The Meaning of the *Islas Dotadas* Episode in the *Libro del Cavallero Cifar*», *HR*, 38 (1970), 56-68.

the *Islas Dotadas* episode in the same way that Berceo explained the meaning of his Introduction to the *Milagros*.

Roboán's struggle with his rebellious vassals after he has returned to Triguida and has become its emperor, which is a continuation of the *Islas Dotadas* episode, should be understood in similar fashion. By giving the treasonous lords names which refer to certain sins (see Chapter Seven), the author suggests the kind of stereotyped battle of virtue against vice which originated in the *Psychomachia*. This section where Roboán triumphs over sin and thereby makes amends for his transgressions in the Islas Dotadas is aesthetically and structurally the resolution of the adventure which occurs in the Fortunate Isles.

Poetic allegory also seems to be found in the Lady of the Lake portion of the first *exemplum* which serves a function similar to that of the section which recounts the revolt against Roboán. Here el Cavallero Atrevido enters the pool into which the ashes of the traitorous Count Nason have been thrown to discover a strange kingdom ruled by a mysterious woman who is a minion of Satan. Although I am not sure in regard to the meaning of the episode, I think it is an allegorical representation illustrating in some manner the evils of treason. As this section could be removed from the work without appreciably altering the meaning of the first *exemplum*, it is likely that the author of the *Zifar* intended it to be a kind of coda summing up allegorically the long section which treats the treason and revolt of Count Nason. Again a *quid pro quo* exegesis appears to provide the most likely way of understanding what the author of the *Zifar* was hoping to demonstrate here. [19]

The reason why the author chose to introduce episodes which can be seen as purely poetic fictions, devised to illustrate and stress certain points which he wished to make, is not clear. The use of the supernatural in these sections does seem to indicate that the reader was expected to sense the difference in atmosphere between these poetic allegories and the figural configurations brought into relief by the *emiendas*. The problems which these episodes seem to treat, treason and *cupiditas*, were the ones viewed in medieval times as most dangerous to the body politic. Of course the «meaning» of these phenomena was negative in connotation as opposed to the positive force of those things in the

[19] See Chapter Seven.

Zifar which the author emphasized as having happened naturally. Perhaps he was hoping to establish a basic good versus bad symbolism by using the kind of allegory for the good which is seen as true while employing the fictive variety to portray the bad.

Since the *Zifar* is founded upon the organizational principles of the medieval university sermon, the ideology behind this rhetorical form should aid us to see what the author was attempting to demonstrate with what seems to be a series of loose typological antitypes and subfulfilments. The sermonic theme of the *Zifar* is the principle *redde quod debes*, the medieval concept which held that man had to return something to God and his fellow man for every thing which he took or was given. The meanings which can be found by adhering to the outline provided by the allegory of name and date must be comprehended within the context of this overall theme. Everything which Zifar and his family accomplish is in some way responsive to the dictum that man should pay what he owes.

The manner in which the Christian could fulfil the principle *redde quod debes*, particularly in regard to God, was a question of great interest to the Middle Ages in that it touched upon the very reason for Creation itself. When God placed Adam and Eve in the Garden of Eden, he expected them to follow certain precepts in return for their having been granted this earthly paradise. They failed to comply and the result was their fall from a state of perfection into one of gross imperfection. The Old Testament Law and, even more important, the Incarnation, death and Resurrection of Christ gave mankind a way of annulling the effects of the Fall and a means of returning to perfection through grace. Again man was placed in a state of obligation to God. In and through Christ he had been given a gift. In order to merit this gift the medieval Christian felt that it was necessary to return something to God. This recompense was in part accomplished through the Sacrifice of the Mass and by means of the worship and glorification of the Trinity which poured forth in the Daily Office. But more than this was felt to be necessary. Through observance of *redde quod debes* in his daily life and through obedience to God's law, medieval man believed that he would attain salvation which in itself was the ultimate fulfilment of this principle in that man was returning his soul to God by means of the gifts given to him. Christ had died on the cross (the gift) so that man might be saved (the recompense). The idea which the Middle Ages continuously preached was that every Christian, because of this divine sacrifice, had a duty in regard to his own salvation and that of his fellow man. The manner in which one could best aid other men toward the glorious afterlife in the celestial city was by observing *redde quod debes* in civil affairs so that justice and peace could be procured for all. Salvation through *redde quod debes* was a communal possibility as well as an individual one. [20]

A work constructed upon the basis of a university sermon is rather difficult for the modern critic to understand and appreciate in that such a sermon was conceived to serve an intellectual bias which has long since disappeared. The medieval university homily was a highly developed rhetorical form, the product of both the Classical orational tradition and the early scholastic dialectic mode of thinking. [21] It gave to the preacher a medium for presenting his ideas which was as fully suited to painstaking thought and intricate argument as was any philosophical *questio*. It was one of the most important of prose genres in early Romance literature [22] and as such was in a ready position to serve as a prototype for creative writing.

The *artes praedicandi*, special tracts composed to aid preachers in constructing sermons, listed rhetorical devices and modes, similar to those familiar to readers of the medieval *artes poeticae*, which could be utilized in forming the dilation or body of a sermon. One of these modes, which well may be the reason for the large number of *exempla* found within the pages of the *Zifar*, directed the preacher to sprinkle his *dilatio* with an ample number of pithy anecdotes to illustrate and stress his points. Another mode was that of expounding the theme according to the four-fold method of allegorical interpretation, [23] while another recom-

---

[20] Thus Juan Manuel says: «Et porque entendí que la salvacion de las almas ha de ser en ley et en estado, por ende convino et non pude excusar de fablar alguna cosa en las leys et en los estados» (*Libro de los estados*, 282).

[21] For bibliography relating to the medieval university sermon see my article in *Viator*.

[22] C. A. Robson, *Maurice of Sully and the Medieval Vernacular Homily* (Oxford, 1952), 27.

[23] The preacher would state the theme with its literal meaning and then proceed to explain it tropologically, giving its moral application to the life of each Christian; then allegorically, stating its significance in regard to the *corpus mysticum* of the Church within history; and finally anagogically when he would relate the theme to the conditions of the celestial kingdom beyond history.

mended the giving of names with allegorical significance to persons and things mentioned in the sermon. Doubtless the author of the *Zifar* was influenced by the methods of dilation expounded in the *artes praedicandi*, although it is difficult to determine just what devices he was copying since those recommended tended to differ from one treatise to another, [24] and also because many of the rhetorical artifices were meant to enhance oral delivery and would have been of little or no use in a work composed to be read.

The most common means recommended for constructing the *dilatio* or *depositio* of a university sermon was for the preacher to take three different aspects of the theme and discuss each of them so as to make the significance clearer to the listeners. It seems reasonable to assume that the three main divisions into which the *Zifar* naturally falls, the «Cavallero de Dios y rey de Mentón» which treats primarily Zifar's adventures, the «Castigos del rey de Mentón» in which Zifar teaches his sons those things which it behooves a ruler to know, and «Los hechos de Roboán» which involves the adventures of the younger son, are three illustrations of the basic theme of the work, *redde quod debes*. To properly understand the work, one must seek to comprehend how these major *exempla* demonstrate the theme and what the author's way of implementing this demonstration was.

Two aspects of the *Zifar* aid us in seeing what the author was attempting to illustrate in the three major *exempla* which he drew from his theme. First, the adventures of both father and son move to happy endings. The tone of the *Zifar* is optimistic; the author seems to be saying that the ills which plague mankind are temporary and solvable provided man strives to retain the grace of God and to use the talents naturally entrusted to him. The manner in which the human race can regain a state of spiritual and physical happiness, lost through the Fall of Adam, is to follow the spirit of *redde quod debes*. If each and every man pays what he owes to his fellow man and to God, human society will slowly perfect itself.

Second, the three major *exempla* are grossly uneven in theme and content—a fact which was probably more important than any other in leading critics to doubt the existence of any organiz-

[24] Otto A. Dieter, «*Arbor Picta*: The Medieval Tree of Preaching», *QJS*, 51 (1965), 142.

ing principle within the work. The first *exemplum*, the redemptive journey of Zifar and his later deeds as king of Mentón, has what I feel to be a comic structure based loosely upon the life of Christ. It begins in adversity but ends in joy. The third *exemplum* is organized around a quest theme which is familiar to readers of the Old French romances. There is no real and pressing reason for Roboán to set out on his journey, as there was for his father, save that he feels within his heart a need to complete this quest as a kind of fulfilment. The adventures of both Zifar and Roboán fall within the sphere of chivalrous action.

The second *exemplum*, in which Zifar instructs his sons in the ways of chivalry and kingship, is very much out of temper with the other two. They are filled with movement and action, while its tenor is static. From the beginning of Zifar's admonitions the author spins out a long and tedious treatise, patched together from various sources, which faithfully echoes the dry atmosphere of the *de regimine principium*. Except for the occasional «otrosy mios fijos» to bring him back, the reader would lose track of himself and forget that he is reading something conceived as a connecting device between the two adventure portions of the work. If, however, the *Zifar* was based upon sermon structure and if the author was conscious of an artistic need to make his major *exempla* illustrative of the far-reaching significance of his theme *redde quod debes*, then this section would have to serve that end as fully as the other two.

In the next four chapters I shall attempt to explain in detail the meaning of each of these three major *exempla*. Since they follow one another in temporal as well as logical succession both on the surface level and on the spiritual stratum, it is simplest to begin with Zifar's departure from Tarid and continue with the progress of the family up to the moment when Roboán and his wife Seringa return to Mentón for their seven-day visit. Such a method will mean that certain phenomena of similar nature will necessarily have to be discussed as they occur in the work while it might have been more fruitful to have dealt with all such similarities together. However, the logical order of the book is more important both from the viewpoint of the sermon structure and from that of the medieval reader who would not have separated his impressions into categories.

CHAPTER FOUR

JOURNEY AS REDEMPTION

The knight Zifar, at the beginning of the first *exemplum*, while explaining to his wife Grima why they have suffered so many misfortunes, tells her that he is descended from a family of kings which had lost its position of power because of the evil actions of one of its members. The knight had been warned by his grandfather that there could be no improvement in the family fortunes «fasta que otro venga de nos que sea contrario de aquel rey, e faga bondat e aya buenas constunbres». (34) Zifar suspects that he himself is the long awaited «otro» who will, by his virtuous deeds, remove the curse of evil hanging over the family. «E sy me Dios faze alguna merçed en fecho de armas, cuydo que me lo faze porque se me venga emientes la palabra de mi avuelo» (34). Since «fecho de armas» is the key expression in the knight's thought, these actions may be expected to take place within the confines of the mode of chivalry. Zifar believes that he can, by means of his mastery of the chivalric arts and his personal virtue, redeem himself and thereby restore his family to the lost position of honor. He must push ahead toward this goal because God has placed in him «algunas cosas señaladas de cavalleria que non puso en cavallero deste tiempo» (33), and because this «demanda» will be beneficial for him and for his family line.

If we look ahead in the work we see that because of his saving the land of Mentón from its attackers, and his subsequent marriage to the daughter of the king and his eventual succession to the throne, Zifar does indeed become a ruler and his family is once again royal. Almost all of Zifar's actions in achieving this goal are eminently moral and can be seen as illustrative of how the strong Christian should behave in this world. But if the adage

55

given by the author of the *Zifar* in the place which corresponds to the *argumentatio* of a sermon is to be taken in the context of the medieval exegetical tradition, the reader must see these actions as more than «right» and «Christian» in the usual sense of the terms.   The author has asked the reader to search for a secondary level of meaning implied and pointed to by the literal story. Zifar's quest, while bearing the scrutiny of the historian, must also allude to a spectrum of meaning which is a «re-creation of truths out of sacred history».

The most usual way in which a medieval writer suggests a secondary stratum is to introduce an expositor who, from within, comments upon various action sequences by giving the «true» meaning of each.   An excellent example of this kind of aid to the reader occurs in the *Queste del saint graal* where hermits sally forth to comment upon and to clarify what happens.   In this way the author of the *Graal* made sure that the reader would follow the line of secondary meaning intended for him.

In the *Zifar* there are two such expositions, albeit very generalized ones, which give the reader an idea of what deeper significance the author might have intended for the work. During the debate between Zifar and el Ribaldo in the hermit's hut, Zifar gives the Augustinian comparison of life to a pilgrimage.   «E non te maravilles en la vida del ome, que atal es commo prigrinaçion.   Quando llegara el pelegrino al lugar do propuso de yr, acaba su peligrinaçion. Asi fas la vida del ome quando cunple su curso en este mundo; que donde adelante non ha mas que fazer» (115).   The author here exhorts us to see the course of Zifar's adventures (and by implication those of his son Roboán) as comparable to the pilgrimage of the soul through the world.   Zifar is «whicheverman», to use Singleton's term, who has been chosen to exemplify the journey of the Christian toward heaven while still in this life. [1]   The author reinforced this implication by the etymological clue apparent in the name of the hero—Zifar, which is similar to the Arabic term for traveler.

A second exposition takes place after Zifar and el Ribaldo have beaten off the attack of the wolves during the night when they are camped in «una torre».   El Ribaldo finds meaning in the series of misadventures which he and his master have been

---

[1]   Charles S. Singleton, *Dante Studies,* II (Cambridge, Mass., 1954-58), 5.

forced to suffer. «... [a]sy va ome a parayso, ca primeramente ha de pasar por purgatorio e por los lugares mucho asperos ante que alla llegue» (133). El Ribaldo gives an anagogical bent to his exposition. The trials of this life presuppose better times on this earth just as those of purgatory mean that eventually the soul must pass into paradise. The reader is being asked to see the adventures of Zifar, until the time when he marries the daughter of the King of Mentón and finally becomes king himself, as a sort of earthly purgatory which will restore his family line as well as improve his own personal fortunes. The concern of the critic is to see how the author of the *Zifar* has conceived this «peligrinaçion» as symbolizing redemption both for the individual knight and for all Christianity as well.

Zifar makes a journey and the author has given us the starting point, mid-point and terminus of that journey. The knight tells the lord of the army which was besieging Galapia that he set out from the kingdom of Tarta (81). Zifar's worst moment, the culmination of his despair, will come in the Kingdom of Falac when he is separated from his wife and children. He will finally cease his traveling and find peace and prosperity in the city of Grades in the kingdom of Mentón. The author, by giving names heavy with symbolic meaning to these three places, has outlined the figural progress which Zifar accomplishes and thereby makes it possible to understand how his journey can stand as a symbol for personal as well as general redemption.

The name of Zifar's evil ancestor who had caused the family to lose its royal position was Tarid which means «expelled» or «banished» in Arabic. [2] It is not difficult for the arabist to see that the root from which Tarid is derived, the verb *tarada* which means to banish or to exile, is also the source for the noun form Tarta. Here the last radical «d» has simply been devoiced to «t». The noun *tarda* meaning expulsion or banishment may be found in any Arabic dictionary. The author of the *Zifar* is telling us that the descendants of Tarid (the expelled one) have been living since his expulsion in Tarta (the place of banishment and exile). [3] Once the etymological force of these two names

[2] As Roger M. Walker has pointed out in «The Genesis of *El Libro del Cavallero Zifar*», *MLR*, 62 (1967), 67.
[3] Berceo speaks of this world as exile in the *Vida de San Millán*: «E exir d'est exilio de malveztat poblado...» (ed. Brian Dutton, 90).

is considered it seems clear that we are being asked to perceive a comparison between King Tarid and Adam. The father of mankind was driven from the terrestrial paradise because of sin; Tarid lost his kingdom for the same reason. Tarta, or land of exile, is comparable to the place where the descendants of Adam have wearily toiled from the moment their forefather lost Eden. Zifar, the wandering counterpart of each and every man who treads the road to heaven or hell through this life, can return the line of kings (the human race) to the happy conditions of the primeval garden. The redemptive journey which he makes from Tarta to Falac to Mentón is at once a very personal one and at the same time symbolic of the movement which the entire human race must make to regain the earthly paradise. But the author of the *Zifar* has implied more with the name Tarta than just expulsion and exile.

The word Tarta, undoubtedly linked with the Arabic verb *tarada*, has an amazing resemblance also to *tartarus* which in Latin meant the infernal regions and which in Christian parlance came to signify limbo or Abraham's bosom, the place where the unbaptised and the Old Testament patriarchs had been consigned. The term is widespread in medieval Christian writings in Latin and its use in the vernacular of Spain is attested in Berceo's *Duelo de la Virgen:* «Todos fueron al tartaro por general sentencia.» [4] Since the word is widely found, it is difficult to believe that the author of the *Zifar*, so conscious of etymological allegorical meaning, would not have been aware that he was using a derivative from Arabic which had a close Romance counterpart.

Zifar leaves Tarta, a land of banishment which is also a place akin to the Christian limbo. The name Tarta, with its overtones of sorrow and exile, could be applied very well to the period of Lent during which such themes predominate in the liturgy of the Church. The Latin counterpart of the name Tarta, *tartarus*, is traditionally associated with Good Friday evening, the time when Christ went down into this unholy place to free the Old Testament Patriarchs. Since both aspects of the word Tarta relate to Holy Week, it seems logical that the author of

[4] Verse 84, line 1. Tartarus as the name for limbo is completely commonplace from early Christian times. St. Augustine uses it for example in his Sermo CLX *De Pascha:* «Voces tartari ad adventum Christi...», *PL,* 39, 2059. Innumerable other examples can be found by scanning material dealing with Easter themes in the *Patrologia Latina.*

the *Zifar* might have wished for us to understand that the knight began his journey at this time.

Grima arrives in the land of Orbín after spending two months on board the ship under the protection of the Virgin (98). The author tells us that the date of her entry into the port of Galán (recovery in Arabic) is the great feast of the Assumption of the Virgin (98). As indicated in the previous chapter, the entire episode, Grima's adventures on the ship, her salvation by the Virgin, and the events afterwards in Orbín, can be seen as a kind of prose paean of praise to the Virgin in the manner of one of Berceo's *Milagros* or Alfonso's *Cantigas*. The author has the ship arrive in Orbín on the day of the Assumption as a tribute to the Virgin for having preserved Grima's life and honor while she was in the hands of the evil merchants.

The Feast of the Assumption falls on August 15. Thus Zifar's wife must have left the port of Mella in the land of Falac about June 15 if she spent two months at sea. On the day of her abduction Zifar, having just lost his two sons, reaches the nadir of his fortune. From this point onward he will begin to move toward a happier life. The period of time between when the knight left Tarta and this day is of critical importance for comprehending the meaning of the journey.

O. B. Hardison has taken the «ritual» pattern so apparent in Classical Greek tragedy and has applied it not only to the development of the Latin and vernacular drama in medieval Europe, but also to the liturgy of Septuagesima and Lent. This «ritual» pattern consists of an *agon-pathos* period of struggle and despair where the movement of the hero's fate is essentially downward. At his lowest point, the protagonist declaims against his sufferings in a *threnos* or lamentation. Shortly afterwards there occurs an *anagnorisis* or new self-awareness on the part of the hero followed by a *peripetia* or turning about in the opposite direction. The hero now begins an upward movement into the *theophany* or period of joy (the word means the appearance of a god) where the problems apparent in the *agon-pathos* stage are resolved. Hardison points out that medieval writers habitually speak of the Mass and the Lenten sequence in terms of a transition from *tristia* to *gaudium* [5] (*tristia-gaudium*

---

[5] *Christian Rite,* 285.

59

being the abbreviated Latin form of the «ritual» pattern) while
Otto Von Simson observes that this change from despair to joy
was common in all aspects of medieval life. [6]

Zifar's journey begins in the sadness and despair of Tarta
and moves to its lowest point with the events in Falac. Just
after the sons are lost Zifar comforts his wife by assuring her
that they are under God's protection: «E porende le devemos
tener en merçed que quier que acaesca de bien o de mejor, ca
el es el que puede dar [despues] de tristeza alegria, e despues de
pesar plazer...» (89). The knight, steadfast in his faith, predicts
the end of the period of *tristia* through which he and his family
have been passing and the subsequent beginning of the *gaudium*.
Shortly afterwards he loses Grima to the merchants and thus
arrives at the extreme limit of his despondency. As one would
expect from knowledge of the ritual pattern, there occurs here
a *threnos*-lamentation which demonstrates that the knight has
reached the end of his strength and is capable of bearing no
more. «Señor Dios, bendito sea el tu nonbre por quanta merçed
me fazes, pero Señor, sy te enojas de mi en este mundo, sacame
del; ca ya me enoja la vida, e non puedo sofrir bien con paçiencia
asy commo solia...» (90). He is distraught and prays that God
will reunite him and his family. Then, with some last reserve
of fortitude, Zifar declares himself willing to bear even more if
God wills. «... pero sy aun te plaze que mayores trabajos pase
en este mundo, fas de mi a tu voluntad; ca aparejado esto de
sofrir que quier que me venga» (91).

This is the low point, but it serves a great purpose for the
suffering knight. Suddenly in the midst of his lament he realizes
that he is capable of continuing in this condition of sorrow and,
like Job, able to persevere patiently until God should see fit to
alleviate his anguish. This self-awareness is enough. «Mas
Nuestro Señor Dios, veyendo la paçiençia e la bondat deste buen
cavallero, enbiole una bos del çielo, la qual oyeron todos los que
y eran... Cavallero bueno... non te desconortes ca tu veras de
aqui adelante que por quantas desaventuras te avenieron que te
vernan muchas plazeres e muchas alegrias e muchas onrras;

[6] Von Simson, 163. John R. Elliot has demonstrated that the medieval *Isaac*
drama had a comic structure. «As long as the drama remained distinctly medieval,
the authors of the Abraham and Isaac plays fitted their dramatic techniques to
this ritual plot» («The Sacrifice of Isaac as Comedy and Tragedy», *SP*, 66, 1969, 47).

e non temas que has perdido la muger e los fijos, ca todo lo abras a toda tu voluntad» (91). This voice from heaven produces the *peripetia*. Zifar leaves Mella and goes to the hut of a hermit on the seashore where he meets el Ribaldo and learns of the plight of the King of Mentón. The voice from heaven, miraculously generated in order to show that this *peripetia* is of divine and not human making, is that of the Holy Spirit. [7]

After Zifar has arrived at the hut on the seashore, the hermit sees in a dream «el cavallero su huesped en una torre mucho alta, con una corona de oro en la cabeça e una pertiga de oro en la mano» (121). This presentiment of the knight's forthcoming elevation to kingship proves beyond any doubt that Zifar has left behind the sadness and anguish of the *tristia* period and is beginning his slow ascension toward the ultimate joy of the theophany. That the heavenly voice, the hermit's vision, and Zifar's decision to sally forth to aid the King of Mentón have been inspired by the Holy Spirit is underlined much later in the work after Zifar has become king of Mentón and el Ribaldo is transformed into el Cavallero Amigo. Zifar remembers the important events which took place at the hermit's hut (122) and sends his former squire back to the place to found a monastery: «... e dizele el monasterio de Santi Espritus». El Cavallero Amigo fulfils his lord's request and then prepares a great celebration. «Despues que fue todo acabado, el Cavallero Amigo fizo pregonar que todos los que quisiesen venir a la fiesta de Santi Espiritus, que era la evocaçion de aquel lugar, por onrra de la fiesta e de aquella buena obra nueva, que les darian seños dineros de oro, e de comer aquel dia» (249).

This *fiesta* referred to here is of course Pentecost, the feast of the Church which commemorates the descent of the Holy Spirit upon the Apostles. Grima had arrived in Galán, the *portus salutaris*, on the greatest feast honoring the Virgin who was responsible for her having reached this port safely. The author of the *Zifar* by his use of the Assumption reinforces the

---

[7] As Hardison says (139), such a *peripetia* is always miraculously generated in order to prove that it is a manifestation of the divine will. It is only proper that Zifar, after being reassured by the celestial voice of the Holy Spirit, should go to the abode of a hermit. The monk or anchorite was traditionally associated with the Holy Spirit during the Middle Ages as is apparent in St. Bonaventure: «...ordo monachalis respondet Spiritu Sancto» (*Hexameron* [Collectio XXII], 160). See also Bloomfield, *Piers Plowman*, 75.

meaning which is apparent in the Virgin's ministrations to Grima while she is on the ship. By the same token it seems likely that the author wished the medieval reader to understand that the beginning of Zifar's period of *gaudium*, which took form and direction at the hermit's hut, was connected with Pentecost, the anniversary of the great visitation upon mankind of the Holy Spirit.

The latest date upon which Pentecost can fall is June 13. If we take «dos meses andido sola dentro en la mar desde el dia que entro en la nave, fasta que arribo al puerto» more or less exactly, it would imply that Grima had left Falac about June 15. Although this day could not be Pentecost itself, it is quite possible for it to fall within the Octave of this Feast during which time there is constant reference in the Mass texts and in the Office to the advent of the Holy Spirit. [8]

Zifar has been in a place which the author wishes to correlate with the idea of banishment (from the Garden of Eden) and the concept of the Christian *tartarus* or limbo. [9] During that week in which the Church commemorates Christ's descent into hell and the subsequent freeing of the Fathers, the knight starts out upon a journey which will redeem his family and, in figure, the whole human race. [10] Easter Sunday which begins the next

---

[8] For example the Introit for the Mass of Tuesday in Pentecost uses 4 Esdras 2.36-37 as a prefigurement of the gift of the Holy Spirit. «Accipite jucunditatem gloriae vestrae, alleluia: gratias agentes Deo, alleluia: qui vos ad caelestia regna vocavit...» The Epistle, Acts 8, 14-17, relates how the Holy Spirit was given to the people of Samaria when Peter and John laid hands upon them. The Octave of Pentecost is more apropos than the day itself as a time of «subfulfilment» in terms of the Holy Ghost because the liturgical texts of the period stress the outpouring of the Spirit upon the whole Christian community in contrast to the first descent upon the Apostles gathered in Jerusalem.

[9] The Fathers were held in limbo during the entire period of the Old Law and were released when the New Law promulgated by Christ's sacrifice was made manifest. Robertson points out that in the Second Shepherd's Play of the Wakefield Cycle «...the sufferings of the shepherds in a cold and stormy world... are not 'reflections of contemporary life'; they are instead typical of the sufferings under the Old Law which any man might experience before he has discovered for himself what St. Paul calls 'the freedom wherewith Christ hath made us free'» (*Preface to Chaucer*, 301). Likewise the author of the *Zifar* probably conceived the sufferings of the knight and his family in Tarta as taking place under the Old Law. Christ's Sacrifice allows him to depart that unhappy place and seek new life.

[10] During the journey of Zifar and his family from Tarta to Falac the author is careful to give the exact interval of time which they spend at each point (Cf. pp. 40, 41, 83, 85, 86). The total number of days is about 57 or 8 weeks if the month which the family spent in Galapia is counted as 30 days. If the day of Zifar's *anagnorisis* and *peripetia* is considered as falling within the Octave of Pentecost, then his departure from Tarta, 57 days before, would have occurred a day or so after Palm Sunday—during Holy Week.

week is the day when Christ rises victorious from the tomb thereby ransoming mankind from original sin. [11] The author of the *Zifar* wishes the reader to see that the knight left Tarta, with the double implication of its name, and began his *demanda* at that very time of the year when the Church recalls Christ's great sacrifice.

In order to understand the broad range of concepts implied here with which the author of the *Zifar* would have expected his medieval reader to be familiar, it is necessary to reiterate that the Christian of the Middle Ages saw the liturgical cycles as recurrences, in a mystical way, of the great events which inaugurated them. Easter was not just the anniversary of Christ's Resurrection. To the medieval mind Christ figurally rose again and again during each and every paschal season for the Redemption of mankind. «The paschal mystery, the death and Resurrection of Christ, is the central theme of the Easter cycle—not merely as a historical commemoration, but as a here-and-now manifestation of His glorification in the Christian assembly». [12]

The Easter celebration was, during the course of early Christianity, slowly extended backward to form a period of preparation which we now know as Septuagesima and Lent. Likewise the Octave of Easter and the following six weeks up to Pentecost developed a particular character which reflected the monumental importance of Christ's Resurrection. The pre-Easter period was also taken figurally to represent this earthly vale of tears and sorrow, while the weeks after Easter were seen as typologically representing the future heavenly kingdom. From St. Augustine «Pâques est la proclamation du règne de l'Agneau...» [13]

Aulén has shown that Septuagesima and Lent in the early Middle Ages were conceived in terms of a struggle, contest or agon. [14] The period recapitulated the great conflict between

---

[11] John Beleth expresses very well the medieval view which combines the motifs of Christ's freeing of the Fathers on Friday with His triumphant Resurrection on Sunday: «Sed cum tartara fregit, et sanctorum animas inde reduxit dieque tertio resurrexit» (*Rationale Divinorum Officiorum, PL,* 97, 202). An antiphon, *ad crucem adornandam,* for Holy Thursday links Christ's Harrowing of Hell directly to our entrance into the heavenly kingdom: «O admirabile pretium, cujus pondere captivitas redempta est mundi. Tartarea confracta sunt claustra inferni, aperta est nobis janua regni» (*Liber Antiphonarius, PL,* 78, 675).

[12] E. Johnson, «Easter and its Cycle», *CE,* 5, 7.

[13] Prosper Guéranger, *L'Année liturgique* (Paris, Poitiers, 1911), 7, 269.

[14] Gustaf Aulén, *Christus victor* (London, 1931), 114.

Christ and the Devil for the fate of mankind. Step-by-step during the long weeks from Septuagesima to Easter morning the Christian participated in the dramatic actions by which Christ made atonement for original sin. Hardison in his chapter «The Lenten Agon» has studied this pre-Easter period of struggle in terms of the drama and has shown how very often military terminology and nomenclature were used to make the conflict even more real. [15]

Aulén admits that by the time of Anselm's *Cur homo deus?* the Roman Church had ceased to look upon Septuagesima-Lent in terms of a conflict or agon and had begun to consider the pre-Easter period either on a purely theological plane or as a time of moral reassessment. But far from Rome and the centers of theological and philosophical disputation the time running up to Easter continued to be seen and experienced in terms of a dramatic contest between Christ and Satan. [16] According to this view Christ, through His great virtue and strength first defeats the Devil during the forty days in the wilderness and later wins final victory in the Resurrection. The Christian can be said to participate vicariously with Christ in effecting this victory over Satan by sharing the great conflict of Lent which leads up to the Crucifixion. The whole point of Christian doctrine is, however, that man was and is incapable alone of annulling the damning effects of original sin. Only the Son of God incarnate is capable of dealing with Satan in both human and supernatural terms. Christ wins the victory of Lent and Easter for man. On Easter morning, with the Resurrection, He hands the gauntlet to all Christianity. He has won for man, and with no aid from man, the metaphysical contest and has invalidated the curse placed upon Adam. But the struggle must now be taken up on the human plane. The worst of sin, original sin, no longer binds us; but Satan can still cause perdition with all the plethora of minor transgressions which he is capable of mustering to his cause.

The Middle Ages, seeing Septuagesima and Lent as a period of struggle between God and Satan for the fate of man, likewise saw the period after Easter as a time of almost equal conflict when the Christian took up the good fight with the Devil in

[15] *Christian Rite,* 80-138.
[16] Aulén, 115.

human terms. In medieval sermons and literary works there are many references to the trials which humanity will face because of Satan's anger over his loss to Christ. «En esta presente historia se cuenta como los diablos fueron muy sanudos quando nuestro señor Jesu Christo fue a los infernos e saco dende a Adan e a Eva y de los otros quantos le plugo». [17]

> Segnor, passez est le Quaresme, passee est le Pasque; li plusor sunt confés e acomenié, deguerpi ont li plusor le diable e ses ovres, pris se sunt a Deu e a sun servise... Kar li diables a ore mult perdu si est dolans de sun damage, se va environ por restorer se perte, e pur trebuchier les homes en pechié... pur ço devuns estre curieus de vos mostrer ses mals engiens, e que vos gardez de ses mals assals e qu'il vos membre de ço que vos avez pramis a Deu, que vos faciez vos penitences e celes ovres par quoi vos soiez sals. [18]

If the Christian to whom Maurice of Sully was speaking were a neophyte newly baptised at Easter, as was the tradition, or a penitent who had been expelled from the Church on Ash Wednesday and readmitted ceremonially on Maundy Thursday, these warnings would be clear and to the point. The neophyte or penitent would have just undergone a rigorous test during Lent somewhat paralleling the historical experience of Christ. But with the end of this test, the new or rededicated Christian had by no means reached the cessation of his struggle with the Devil. In fact he would now be doubly put upon by the demonic troup angry because of Christ's victory and anxious to return the Christian to the paths of sin.

By the 10th century infant baptism began to reduce the number and importance of the catechumens during the period of Lent leaving only a few, together with the odd penitent, to pass through the pre-Easter trial. [19] The Church was left with a great number of nominal Christians, baptised as infants, who were free from the stain of original sin and who had done nothing so grievously wrong since baptism so as to merit expulsion from the Church on Ash Wednesday. But the majority of those in the Christian fold were always in dire need of spiritual renovation.

So another aspect of the Easter pageant, implicit all along,

---

[17] *El baladro del Sabio Merlín* in *Libros de Caballerías*, I, 3.
[18] Sermon 16, Maurice de Sully, Robson, 116-117.
[19] Hardison, 95.

comes to the fore and gains great importance in medieval thinking. Writers began to emphasize the Paschal season as a time of renewal when the Christian, once again reminded that the historical Christ had freed him from original sin in a comparable season in the past, should seek more vigorously in life the road which would lead him after death to the New Jerusalem. This idea is very clearly expressed in the liturgy: «Domine sancte, Pater omnipotens, aeterne Deus: qui nos per paschale mysterium docuit vetustatem vitae relinquere, et novitate spiritus ambulare...» [20] The Christian, mystically freed at Easter from the constrictions of the Old Law, should attempt to take fullest advantage of this «new life» by redoubling his struggles with the Devil while at the same time trying to move spiritually closer to God. «Venite, benedicti Patris mei, percipite regnum, alleluia, quod vobis paratum est ab origine mundi». [21]

The Easter season is, of course, the archetypal time par excellence for beginning anything anew. It comes in the spring when the earth itself is escaping from the death of winter. The Middle Ages (as the Church still does) looked upon the Paschal time as the part of the year when Adam was formed in the Garden of Eden, and, more important, as the season when the general Resurrection preceding the Day of Judgment would occur. [22] Historically the Children of Israel had escaped from Pharaoh's hordes in this period by crossing the Red Sea and fleeing toward the Promised Land. The Middle Ages never grew tired of dwelling upon the Easter «meanings», drawing them out into all sorts of complicated figures.

The departure of the Children of Israel under Moses for example particulary caught the imagination of medieval religious thinkers and they interpreted this flight mystically as applying still to them. Dante in his letter to Can Grande expresses this concept:

> Now if we attend to the letter alone the departure of the children of Israel from Egypt in the time of Moses is presented to us; if the allegory, our redemption wrought by Christ; if the moral sense, the conversion of the soul from the grief and misery of sin to the

[20] Feria V in albis, *Liber Sacramentorum*, PL, 78, 95.
[21] Feria quarta of Easter Week, *Liber Antiphonarius*.
[22] Guéranger, 8, 71-72.

state of grace; if the anagogical, the departure of the holy soul from the slavery of this corruption to the liberty of eternal glory. [23]

The individual Christian of course could take no active part in the application of any of these senses to his life; they had all been accomplished simultaneously for him through Christ's death and Resurrection. The only thing that each man alone could do under his own power was to participate in an action which would recall and somehow fulfil Christ's sacrifice. This human action could not be like Christ's (how can any man be like Christ?) but it could imitate what Christ had done since imitation does not imply that the essence of the imitated object is present in the imitator. The medieval imagination was perfectly free to recapitulate the «meaning» of the sacrifice of the historical Jesus into the lives of everyman or «whicheverman». In fact, since medieval man looked upon this «meaning» as constant and ever-recurring, he was obliged to find it in events around him. Christ's death and Resurrection was the central event in Christian thought and one would expect the form and result of this event (recurring annually as a reminder) to be reflected in some manner in the life of every person who believed it.

This is what the author of the *Zifar* is attempting to demonstrate in the first major *exemplum* of his work. He is showing how the outline of Christ's great deed is constantly to be perceived in the life of the individual Christian, particularly in that season of the Church year which recalls Jesus' example. Instead of being an Easter poem of the redemption of man, as Alfred Jacob considers *The Divine Comedy* and the *Razón de amor*, [42] «El Cavallero de Dios» is a prose *exemplum* of the redemption of man. Through the mode of the ritual formula the author leads us to see how Zifar removes the curse from his family and how his hardships purify him and make him worthy of an exalted position. These actions of the knight have deep signi-

[23] Trans. Singleton, *Dante Studies*, I, 14. This sort of interpretation must have been commonplace in the Middle Ages. The same kind of explanation of the «meaning» of Easter as a season can be found in a sermon by Garnerius who was abbot of Clairvaux about 1195: «...quia Pascha *transitus* interpretatur, tanquam invitati ad coelestes nuptias transeamus, de tenebris ad lucem, de infidelitate ad fidem, de vitiis ad virtutem, de morte ad vitam, vel de mundo ad Patrem, ut sic in voce exsultationis et confessionis in primo celebramus Pascha historicum, in secundo allegoricum, in tertio tropologicum, in quarto anagogicum» (PL, 205, 685).

[24] «The *Razón de amor* as Christian Symbolism», HR, 20 (1952), 286.

ficance for him and for his family; they also have great importance
for all men because the «meaning» of these actions in their totality
has to be taken as an imitation, a recapitulation, and a recurrence
of an archetypal «meaning», the one established by Christ's life
and subsequent death on the cross for the redemption of mankind.
Zifar leaves Tarta which is a figure for exile, banishment, and
limbo. He leaves at the very time of the year when the whole
drama of the redemption in rememoration is moving toward
a climax which will again mystically release man from the vale
of sorrows and project him into the light. [25]

A clue to the reasoning which lies behind the choosing of
Holy Week as the time of departure for Zifar's journey can be
found in a sermon, probably by Hugh of St. Victor, for the Mass
of Palm Sunday. Hugh compares the ten plagues which Moses
unleashed upon Egypt to the Ten Commandments. Just as the
ten plagues failed to convince Pharaoh that he should release
the Children of Israel from the bondage of Egypt, so the
observance of the Ten Commandments was not sufficient to
cause the Devil to free the people of God from their servitude
in the Egypt of this world.

> Et nota quod Moyses in virga decem plagis Pharaonem et Aegytum
> percussit: quibus quidem affligitur, sed donec immoletur agnus non
> vincitur, quia Christus in legis disciplina tanquam in virga decem
> praeceptis quasi decem plagis suo captivari repugnare jubet populo
> Dei, quem diabolus in libertate paradisi conditum in Aegypto
> hujus mundi captivum tenuit; sed sicut Pharao decem plagis non
> adeo vincitur ut filios Israel dimitteret, sic et diabolus decem praecep-
> torum observatione non adeo superatus est, ut homo in paradisum
> rediret. [26]

Hugh is not looking upon the Ten Commandments in a negative
sense but considers them like the ten plagues, an instrument
which was not sufficient to accomplish the hoped-for purpose
because it was too dependent upon human actions. Only a
completely divine agent such as the death angel carrying away
the firstborn of the Egyptians or the Son of God dying upon the
cross could fully accomplish what was yearned for. So eventually .

[25] As Guéranger says: «L'Eglise célèbre l'époque de l'été et de la réconciliation
ou du retour, à partir de l'octave de Pâques jusqu'à l'octave de la Pentecôte...»
(8, 141).
[26] PL, 177, 884.

the Children of Israel are freed and finally mankind is redeemed from the curse of Adam. «At ubi Agnus Dei Christus immolatus est in morte primogenitum Pharaonis, id est originale peccatum deletum est in mari Rubro baptismi Christi sanguine rubentis, actualia quoque peccata cum illo altero penitus absorpta sunt, Dei populo liberato.» Hugh presents the freeing of the Israelites as a figure foreshadowing the redemption of humanity.

Now the cause of Zifar's troubles in Tarta was the fact that no horse or other beast which he owned lived longer than ten days after coming into his possession. The great expense thus incurred by the king of Tarta in maintaining the hardy knight gave «los enbidiosos losengeros», courtiers jealous of Zifar's prowess, a way to undermine his position with the king (13). At the urging of these envious advisors and because of the expense the king ceased using Zifar in his wars although he was by far the best of his knights.

What the author of the *Zifar* has done here is cleverly to combine two motifs which the medieval mind saw as central to the theme of man's fall and subsequent redemption. The first is that medieval writers often viewed the tempter in the Garden of Eden not as a serpent but as «mesongeros» or «losengeros» who, by lying to Eve, cajole her into tasting the forbidden fruit. [27] The «enbidiosos losengeros» in the kingdom of Tarta repeat the archetypal action performed in the Garden of Eden and thereby cause Zifar, symbolic descendant of Adam and Eve, to be driven from Tarta. [28] God has used the pattern of deception and expulsion, which resulted first in man's fall, as a means of restoring him to happiness.

The second point, likewise a reversal of symbolism, is that the death of the livestock after ten days refers to the ten plagues, which were ineffectual against Pharaoh, and to the Ten Commandments which Hugh has shown to have been largely useless against original sin. Observance of the Ten Commandments did not release man from spiritual bondage and the ten plagues did not result in freedom for the Children of Israel, but the curse of the death of his livestock after ten days will cause Zifar to

---

[27] See for example Gonzalo de Berceo's, *Loores de Nuestra Señora,* 4abc, and *Duelo de la Virgen,* 83d.

[28] As is the case in the *Cantar de Mio Cid* where the Cid loses his place with the king for the same reason: «Por malos mestureros de tierras sodes echados» (267).

depart from the earthly Egypt, Tarta, where he lingers in the shadows of unrenewed life. Just as the wood of the cross typologically fulfils and reverses the effects of the wood of the Tree of Life in the Garden of Eden, so the ten-day curse fulfils and accomplishes what the ten plagues and the Ten Commandments did not. Zifar leaves his «Egypt» while the Children of Israel had to wait for the angel of death to effect their delivery. The important point is that because historically the first Passover and its fulfilment, the death of Christ on the cross, have already occurred before Zifar's time in Tarta, the antitype *anno domini* of the ten plagues and Ten Commandments (the ten-day curse) can be now effective. Christ's sacrifice allows the departure of man from the Egypts of this world whenever he chooses to set out. He no longer has to wait for a divine agent to release him from his captivity. Jesus' example is there to lead him to the promised land whenever he wishes to follow.

Hugh mentions the ten plagues of Egypt, the death angel, and the departure of the Children of Israel in his Palm Sunday sermon because he sees these events as foreshadowing the Passion of Christ. Just as the original Passover lamb was to be brought forth on the tenth day of the month (Exodus 12.3) so Christ on Palm Sunday at the time of the tenth moon enters Jerusalem to be immolated for the sake of mankind. «Dominica in ramis Palmarum qua Dominus Jerusalem passurus intravit, illa decima exstitit, quia praeceptum erat in lege, ut decima die tolleretur agnus.» [29] Palm Sunday thus recalls the bringing forth of the original Passover sacrifice which was ultimately to result in the freeing of the Children of Israel from the bondage of Egypt. The Palm Sunday procession, habitually made in churches throughout the West, had symbolically bound up in it all the implication of the first Passover, the subsequent fleeing of the Children of Israel from Egypt, and the fulfilment of these Old Testament types, the entry of Christ into Jerusalem. It was considered to be a figured representation of Christ's divine mission to earth. «Haec autem processio praesignat quae utilitas sit in sanguine ipsius, et quis fructus passionis ex illa misericordia, in cujus multitudinem benedictus advenit.» In the same way that the reading of the entire Passion of Christ during the Palm

[29] *PL*, 177, 884.

Sunday Mass previews the events which historically took place during the following week in Jerusalem and which were thereafter commemorated in the liturgy of Holy Week, so the Palm Sunday procession in the Middle Ages alluded to Christ's entire mission to mankind, His descent from the Father, His time on earth, and His return to heaven.

It is doubtless for this reason that the author of the *Zifar* fixed the moment of the knight's leaving Tarta as the days after Palm Sunday. By doing so he could equate Zifar's redemptive journey on the plane of human action with Christ's divine errand to humanity. He could present the ideal toward which conscientious medieval Christians were constantly striving in their lives—the *imitatio Christi*. [30]

An excellent example of the way in which the medieval saw Christ's life as exemplary for each and every individual is found in two sermons by Richard of St. Victor under the heading in Migne *Tractatus de gemino paschate*. [31] In the first of the sermons, written for Palm Sunday, Richard tells us that Easter should be considered as double or twinned. «Geminum pascha colimus, geminum sane celebrare debemus» (1059). He defines these «two» Easters in terms of movement, «transitus»; «Quid ergo dicimus pascha floridum, nisi transitum honestum et gratum? Quid ergo dicimus pascha fructiferum, nisi transitum jucundum et moni gaudio plenum?» (1059). Richard has gotten his idea of a doubled *transitus* through observance of the pattern of Christ's life on earth and in heaven.

> Geminum processionem Christus fecit, geminam sane facere nos voluit: *Exivi*, inquit, *a Patre, et veni in mundum*; interum relinquo

[30] «The importance of the journey which is an imitation of Christ cannot be underestimated for the Middle Ages, for it consists of a pattern based on Christ's life in the scheme of redemption and was seen to be evident in both the Old and New Testament and in the liturgy as well» (Levy, 73). Dorothy Donnelly explains how the medieval viewed Christ's life as a journey: «Jesus Christ, who shared our nature shared its patterns of action; and thus it was that His life in time, like every human life, approximated to the pattern of a journey. In the beginning was the Word, and that must be the very beginning of the story, but 'once upon a time', as the tales say, the Word, that is the Son, went out from the Father's kingdom and the Father's house. He entered into a dark forest. When the appointed time came He went out, of His own Free Will, into the wild desert to meet His trial, and here He overcame His enemy, the devil, even as the tale's hero overcame the beast. As was so often the case in the imaginative tales, this was but a preliminary encounter and not the final, or great trial» (*The Golden Well*, London, 1950, 166).

[31] *PL*, 196, 1060-1074.

mundum, et vado ad Patrem (Joan, xvi). A summo coelo egressio
ejus, haec est processio prima; et occursus ejus usque ad summum
ejus, haec est processio secunda. Primo descendit, postea ascendit.
Prima processio est humiliationis, secunda est exaltationis. Si vere
Christiani sumus Christum imitari debemus. Qui enim se dicit in
Christo manere, debet sicut Christus ambulavit et ipse ambulare.
Primo humiliemur cum Christo ut postmodum exaltemur cum
Christo. (1060-61)

Basically the movement of these two processions described by
Richard, if viewed together, forms the familiar ritual pattern of
pathos-peripetia-theophany. Christ begins the descending action
when he humbles himself to be incarnate as a human. After the
descent from heaven at the moment of Incarnation, the first
33 years, or 32 if we adhere to a prevalent medieval tradition, of
Christ's life stretch out on an even plane. It is not until the very
last, during the forty days in the wilderness when the Son of God
is tempted and hounded by Satan himself, that the pattern of
Jesus' life takes a downward turn. The action sequence levels
off briefly after the temptation to spiral toward its lowest point
on that Thursday when He was betrayed. After the Crucifixion,
the pathos period reaches its nadir as the Son of God descends
from the tomb to visit the nether regions of hell in order to deliver
the imprisoned patriarchs. The Resurrection is the *peripetia*.
By humbling Himself to suffer such a series of awful experiences,
Christ triumphs. The *theophany* or *gaudium* period continues
from Easter morning until the Ascension when Christ is exalted
back to the Father from Whom He descended.

Richard of St. Victor is telling the Christian that he must
imitate this action of Christ; he must be humbled to the greatest
degree before he can be exalted. The author of the *Zifar*'s plan
for the knight's redeeming journey is very similar to the dual
procession of descent-ascent which Christ made.[32] Zifar's family
lost (descended from) its high position because of the evil actions
of Tarid which were willingly committed since man is free to

---

[32] Maurice of Sully in a sermon for Palm Sunday also compares the real procession
which the faithful made on that day to the spiritual advancement which they should
undertake at the Easter season. «...donques saciés bien que vos avés faite la
procession que Dex aime e que lui plaist; e se vos ne l'avés issi faite propensés
vos, amendés vos, trespassés de mal en bien, e de bien en miels—e si vos apareilliés
en ceste sainte semaine qui est a venir, en tel maniere que dignement puisiés venir
le jor del juise a la grant procession quant tote saint Eglise trespassera de cest monde
el ciel...» (Robson, 112).

do wrong if he chooses. The family remains in an inferior position until Zifar is able to reverse the effect of his ancestor's actions by imitating in human terms the redemptive pattern presented by Christ. Zifar's grandfather had made clear to him as a child the sequence of events which would be necessary to restore the family. «... vuestro linaje e nuestro cobre, fasta que otro venga de nos que sea contrario de aquel rey, e faga bondat e aya buenas costunbres...» (34). Once Christ had prepared the way for this «otro», the restoration of the family (mankind) could take place. Zifar's elevation to the kingship of Mentón is the exaltation of the family line; the final uplifting of humanity itself, figured by the knight's rise, would have to wait until the Second Coming for its complete restitution, but it could partially be accomplished on earth by the establishment of kingdoms where truth and justice would prevail.

After Richard of St. Victor has described Christ's descending-ascending action, he shifts his frame of reference. He has said that Christ's descent from heaven, His humility in suffering the human condition, His passion and death, should be imitated by «whicheverman» so that he could, in the end, follow Christ in His return to heaven. [33] But in order to do this, the Christian would have to have a means possible within the context of human experience which would still resemble the divine model. The comparison which Richard proposed would have to be explained in terms relevant to human life if it were to be understood and, more important, if it were to be imitated. Richard solves this dilemma by making Jesus' short journey from Bethany to Jerusalem, on what is to be Palm Sunday, a figure for Christ's whole descending-ascending sequence which he has described. The physical trip from Bethany to Jerusalem is made to reflect the essence of meaning implied in the metaphysical journey from heaven to earth and back again. The Christian cannot imitate Christ by descending from heaven and then returning there triumphant; but he can follow the idea of a real journey which Jesus made on earth. From Bethany through the Mount of Olives to Jerusalem becomes for Richard «ex obedientia per pietatem, cum humilitate ad pacem». [34] He accomplishes this by

[33] As Isaac of Stella advises Christians in one of his Easter sermons: «Quod in nobis adimplere dignetur is, cujus resurrectionem colimus et imitamur, quoad possumus...» (PL, 194, 1827).
[34] PL, 196, 1065.

interpreting the etymological meanings of the names. Bethany in Hebrew is obedience. *Olivetum* in Greek is *misericordiam* «... et ipsam oleum opera pietatis designat» (1062). The ass upon which Christ sits stands for humility and, finally, Jerusalem is *visio pacis*. This vision of peace is to be understood as corresponding not only to that final peace of the celestial Jerusalem but also to earthly *pax* which can be achieved through brotherhood. All of this refers to «... processio Christi, quam imitari debent Christiani» (1061).

Richard has thus explained to the medieval Christian, by means of the figure of the trip from Bethany to Jerusalem, how he can imitate Jesus. In obedience he must begin his earthly journey; he must humble himself severely while performing works of mercy during the entirety of his wandering. Finally he will arrive at his destination, a place of eternal peace and rejoicing.

In another sermon for Easter Day, which follows this one, Richard tells us that «una igitur resurrectio Domini secundum carnem, geminam nostram resurrectionem efficit, et animarum in presenti... et resurrectionem corporum in futura».[35] Just as Christ underwent a double procession, a descending-ascending sequence, which we are to imitate by descending through obedience to humility and then rising to peace, so our reward, our «resurrection» is twofold also—one on this earth, the other in heaven. We can only look forward to that resurrection which will place us in heaven, but we can actively take part in the one meant for us here. «Jam nos igitur innovati, et in novitate vitae positi ambulemus de novitate in novitatem, de claritate in claritatem, de virtute in virtutem: nam in eadem virtute de gradu in gradum procedimus» (1071).

Richard conceives our present spiritual resurrection not in mystical terms but as a physical movement from evil to good.

> Quis enim dicit se in Christo manere, debet sicut et ipse ambulavit et ipse ambulare, hoc est eum imitari, et ideo imago ab imitando scilicet, gloria Dei, ut Deus non ipse vir per omnia glorificetur.

[35] *Ibid.*, 1071. Durandus in his *Rationale* expresses much the same idea: «De plus, le Christ n'eut qu'une seule résurrection, c'est-à-dire la résurrection de son corps, qui désigne un nombre de deux; mais, pour nous, nous avons une double résurrection, savoir: la résurrection de l'ame, du pêché; et la résurrection du corps, de la corruption...» (trans. Charles Barthélemy III, Paris, 1854, 279).

Hanc eamdem processionem Dominus designat, ubi ait: Surge tolle grabatum tuum, et vade in domum tuam (Marc. II). (1073)

The idea that the Christian should make a *transitus* at Easter, foreshadowed not only by the escape of the Children of Israel from Egypt but also by events in Christ's life, was a metaphor not at once comprehensible in all its complexity. What the author of the *Zifar* did was to incorporate all the meaning of this *transitus* which Richard expresses as physical movement, with its plethora of implications ranging from Adam to the celestial Jerusalem, under the symbol of a knight's journey from the exile and unhappiness of Tarta to the exaltation of Mentón. The knowledgeable reader would have been expected to understand that this journey was recapitulating the flight of the Children of Israel and Christ's errand to humanity, as well as suggesting the hoped-for spiritual renovation of each and every Christian at Easter. [36] The author wished his reader to see that there is a «meaning» in all of these events which recurs in the lives of individual Christians and which was basic to the medieval conception of the world.

The pattern of Zifar's journey begins in Tarta at the end of Lent, reaches its lowest point in Falac after Pentecost, and moves to completion in the land of Mentón. The knight has heard the *exsurge* resounding through the Lenten liturgy and obedient to it has left the shadows of exile to seek new life by aiding others. [37] The name of the kingdom of Falac where Zifar's real and spiritual journey reaches its nadir, means «crack», «split»

[36] This is not to state that the author of the *Zifar* knew Richard and was following him, although that of course would not be impossible. I am suggesting that he and Richard subscribed to a view of the drama of the Redemption of man which was common in the Middle Ages. The basic idea of Christ's descent-ascent forming a pattern for man is derived from Ephesians 4. 8-11: «Wherefore he saith, when He ascended up on high, he led captivity captive, and gave gifts unto man» (verse 8). The currency of the idea is shown by Berceo's use of it in the *Loores de Nuestra Señora:* «Si tú non deçendieses yo nunqua non sobria...» (97).
[37] The *exsurge* is heard in the Mass several times during the Lenten season: for example, the Graduals for the Third Sunday, the Tuesday of the Fourth Week and in the one for Monday of Holy Week. The word *exsurge* of course comes from the particular Psalm which is the source of the responsorium for the day. In the Mass it is doubtless an appeal to Christ for His Resurrection which will free mankind from the darkness of original sin symbolized by the period of Lent. It is not difficult to imagine, however, that the individual Christian, hearing the word ring forth during the Mass might have imagined it as being addressed directly to him—an appeal for him to cast off his sins and enter into the new life. This is the interpretation which Helinandus Frigidimontis, a monk who died about 1127 in Flanders, gave to the *exsurge* in his Sermo XIII *In Pascha:* «Exsurge, id est ex terra usque

or «crevice» in Arabic, and is thus appropriate for the place where he is separated in the manner of a Byzantine romance from his family. The word has other implications for the student of Arabic literature which are more fitting to the ritual pattern of Christ's earthly mission which seems to serve as model for Zifar's adventures. To the medieval mind the lowest point of Jesus' experience would have been that period when he went to hell to triumph over Satan by freeing the captive Fathers. After this occurs the *peripetia* of the Resurrection. Now the word *falq* or *falaq* in Moslem eschatological legends was closely associated with the idea of hell and was even viewed as one of the antechambers of that unholy place. [38] It is thus not unlikely that the author of the *Zifar*, familiar enough with the colloquial idiom of the Mozarabs and Mudejars to use it for allegorical puns, might have also known the various legends concerning the afterlife which had wide currency among the Spanish Arabs. His use of the word *falaq* to designate the kingdom where Zifar suffers his worst moment would have equated this place on the plane of human action with hell where Christ realized his great victory over Satan.

Tarta is exile; Falac is the equivalent in human terms of hell. It now remains to explain what the author of the *Zifar* wished to imply by means of the name Mentón. The significance of Grades, the city where the aged King of Mentón is besieged with his daughter, is not difficult to find. The author interprets the name himself: «... e dizenle asy porque esta en alto e suben por

ad coelum surge, quaerendo quae sursum sunt... Respondet Christianus: *Exsurgam diliculo,* id est mox ut sol justitiae mihi ortus fuerit, et radiis gratiae suae mentem meam afflaverit: ut a terra me suspendat, ut post se me trahat, ut ad coelum me pertrahat...» *(PL,* 212, 588-591).

[38] «Under the sea the Lord created a vast abyss of air, under the air fire, and under the fire a mighty serpent, by name Falak; and were it not for fear of the Most Highest, this serpent would assuredly swallow up all that is above it...» (Night 496 of the *Arabian Nights.* Richard Burton, *The Book of the Thousand and One Nights,* reprinted and ed. L. C. Smithers, London, 1894). In night 497 God places hell in the mouth of this serpent Falak. The tradition that hell was to be presented as a serpent is also common in Christian iconography. Northrop Frye, «The Typology of 'Paradisus Regained'», *MP,* 53 (1955-56), points out that the precise moment of Christ's agon with Satan is usually presented in the time between His death and Resurrection while he is harrowing hell: «...hell is usually represented as leviathan, a huge, open-mouthed monster into which, or whom Christ descends...» (228). «*Al-Falq* o la quebranza» is given as the name of a chamber of hell by M. Asín Palacios, *La escatología musulmana en la divina comedia* (3rd ed., Madrid, 1961), 162. *Al-falaq* appears as a well *(pozo)* of hell in *Tradiciones de Mahoma y otros sobre premios y castigos por hacer o dejar de hacer la oración,* ed. Othmar Hegyi (unpublished doctoral thesis, University of Toronto, 1969), 51.

gradas alla» (117). These steps are doubtless the steps of virtue mentioned by Richard of St. Victor, «... nam in eadem virtute de gradu in gradum procedimus». [39] That the figure is a common one is demonstrated by its occurrence in the Preface or Inlatio of the Mozarabic Mass for Pentecost in connection with the reason why there are seven weeks between Easter and Pentecost: «Hi sunt sine dubio septem gradus templi tui: per quos ad celorum regna conscenditur.» [40] The name of the city Grades is evocative of the spiritual renovation which Zifar is slowly undergoing as he proceeds to save Mentón from its attackers. The name of the kingdom of Mentón in which Grades is situated must also be etymologically fitting to the author of the *Zifar*'s drama of the Redemption.

D. W. Robertson has correctly observed that «Any pilgrimage during the Middle Ages... was ideally a figure for the pilgrimage of the Christian soul through the world's wilderness toward the celestial Jerusalem». [41] Richard of St. Victor made the earthly Jerusalem to which Christ traveled on Palm Sunday not only a figure for the celestial city but also for a city of peace upon this earth. «... habemus pacem cum omnibus, et usque ad Jerusalem pervenimus». [42] Likewise the author of the *Zifar* has made Mentón—the end of his hero's journey—a symbol for Jerusalem, the *visio pacis*, the city which we attain when we have peace on earth.

Mentón is the Old Spanish derivative of Latin *mentum* «chin» or «beard». That the author was indeed aware of this meaning seems to be borne out by several puns which he makes in regard to the aged ruler of Mentón. El Ribaldo explains to Zifar that the attacking army will not leave off the siege until its leader «tomase al rey por la barva» (168). The same threat is also voiced by members of the army to Zifar. «Bien creedes que lo non faremos fasta quel tomemos por la barva» (144). This pun has to do with the medieval custom of affronting one's enemy by grabbing and pulling the tip of his beard. [43] But in the context of spiritual renewal during Zifar's *transitus*, the author must have meant something different.

[39]   *PL*, 196, 1071.
[40]   *Missale Mixtum, PL*, 85, 618-619.
[41]   *Preface to Chaucer*, 373.
[42]   *PL*, 196, 1061.
[43]   See Burke, «Names and the Significance of Etymology», 167-168.

The beard was often used by medievals to imply strength, virility, and courage. It was obviously necessary for the king or knight, whose duty was the defense of the realm, to possess these qualities. There was, however, another tradition involving the beard which reinforced the natural tendency to associate it with the protection of the commonwealth. This tradition derived from a striking image taken from Psalm 132v. «Ecce quam bonum, et quam jucundum, habitare fratres in unum. Sicut unguentum in capite, quod descendit in barbam, barbam Aaron.»

From the time of St. Augustine, and most certainly earlier, Psalm 132v was a song extolling the benefits of the communion of saints, not only that forthcoming heavenly communion but also the brotherhood which should exist among Christians upon this earth. This is clearly implied in the Bishop of Hippo's commentary on this Psalm.

> Sed qui sunt qui habitant in unum? Illi de quibus dictum est, *Et erat illis anima una et cor unum in Deum*: *et nemo dicebat aliquid suum esse, sed erant illis omnia communio* (Ac. IV, 32). Designati sunt, descripti sunt, qui pertineant ad barbam... Barba significat fortes; barba significat juvenes, strenuous, impigros, alacres. [44]

St. Augustine sees the *barba* of Psalm 132v as a figure for those strong, enduring Christians, united as one body in Christ, who can, by working together, bring about the kingdom of God upon the earth. Probably following the Bishop of Hippo, the *barba* of Psalm 132v becomes a powerful symbol of that Christian harmony, peace and unity which will characterize not only the heavenly Jerusalem but also its earthly image. In all cases the basis of this meaning remains the identification of the beard with strength and virility.

Peter Lombard in his exposition of Psalm 132v presents the figure in almost precisely the same manner: «... venit Spiritus Sanctus in barba ejus, id est in fortes, strenuous, alacres: quos barba significat... Hi sunt perfecti quin unum habitant, qui legem Christi implent...» [45] Alanus de Insulis makes the connection exact by stating that *barba* means the people of God. «... id est unguentum divinae gratiae, quod descendit a Patre

[44] PL, 37, 1729-1736.
[45] PL, 191, 1183.

in caput, id est in Christum; et a capite in barbam, id est in
populos, quo dicuntur Dei barba, id est fortitudo...» [46]

It would seem logical to assume that Psalm 132v and the
figure of the *barba* were widely accepted as signifying strong
Christian unity and, more important, as implying the benefits
which could and would accrue to mankind once it learned to
dwell in peaceful unity. [47]   In essence *barba* has the same meaning
as Jerusalem or *visio pacis* as described by Richard of St. Victor. [48]
Once the Christian community has reached this Jerusalem, it
would have achieved again what it first lost through the sin of
Adam.

When the knight and his squire reach Mentón, they find that
they cannot enter the city because the besieging army has it
completely surrounded (136). [49]   Zifar resorts to a ruse in order
to attempt to pass the sentries.   After having changed clothes
with el Ribaldo, he places a «guirnalda de fojas en la cabeça»
and approaches the guards.   The action sequence at this point
is very interesting.

> E quando entraron por la hueste començaron a dar bozes al cavallero
> todos, grandes e pequeños, commo a sandio e deziendo: «Ahe

[46]   *Distinctiones, PL,* 210, 718.   This explanation is preceded by the section from
Psalm 132v to which I am referring.

[47]   That the beard from Psalm 132v held meaning beyond the ecclesiastical vale
for medieval Spaniards is demonstrated in *Libro de buen amor,* 374, where in the
beginning of his parody on the canonical hours Juan Ruiz quotes the words *Ecce
quam bonum.*   Otis Green says that the phrase is used in parody to suggest the
raucous fellowship of the tavern *(Spain and the Western Tradition,* I, 54).   The
Archpriest has thus played upon the meaning of the image as a referent for Christian
communion and has converted it into one implying a more earthly kind of sodality.
Psalm 132v was the favorite of the Templars due to its suggestion of earthly
brotherhood.   Because of the mention of Aaron's beard there, the hirsute chin
became the symbol of their organization.   See G. Legman, *The Guilt of the Templars*
(New York, 1966), 131.

[48]   *PL,* 196, 1065.

[49]   El Ribaldo mentioned to Zifar while they were debating at the hermit's
hut, that the kingdom of Mentón was ten days distant (119).   If we take the day
of Zifar's arrival at the hermit's hut to be June 15 (two months prior to Grima's
entrance into Orbín on August 15), then the knight would have left for Mentón
on June 17 as he spent two nights in the hut.   The date of his arrival in Mentón ten days later would have been June 26, the Feast of Saints John and Paul.
Dorothy Donnelly explains that this Feast was dedicated in the Middle Ages to
the idea of brotherhood: «The brotherhood of men which begins in this world
and is perfected in the next is illustrated in the lives and deaths of such martyrs
as John and Paul...» *(The Golden Well,* 190).   The gradual for the Mass of these
martyred brothers is interesting because it contains the verse «Ecce quam bonum»
from Psalm 132v.   It is thus possible that the author of the *Zifar* meant us
to understand that the knight reached Mentón on a day which itself symbolized
brotherhood.

aqui el rey de Menton, syn caldera e syn pendon». Asy que aqueste ruydo andido por toda la hueste, corriendo con el e llamandole rey de Menton. E el cavallero, commoquier que pasava grandes verguenças, fazia enfinta que era sandio, e yva saltando e corriendo fasta que llego a una choça do vendien vino e mal cozinado, que estava en cabo de la hueste e contra los muros de la villa. (137)

Zifar sits down in the tavern and demands that bread and wine be brought to him. Meanwhile el Ribaldo follows his master to the inn and when he finds him there begins to mock and ridicule him.

> El serviente venia en pos el a trecho, deziendo a todos que era sandio, e fuese a la choça do vendian el vino e dixo: «O sandio rey de Menton, aqui eres? Has comido oy?» «Çertas», dixo el sandio, «non». «E quieres que te de a comer por amor de Dios?», dixo el ribaldo. Dixo el sandio: «Querria». Metio mano el serviente a aquello que vendian mal cozinado, e diole de comer e bever quanto quiso. E dixo el serviente: «Sandio, agora que estas beodo cuydas que estas en tu regno?» «Çertas», dixo el sandio.
> E dixo el tavernero: «Pues sandio, defiende tu regno». «Dexame dormir un rato», dixo el sandio, «e veras commo me yre luego a dar pedradas con aquellos que estan tras aquellas paredes». «E commo», dixo el tavernero, «el tu regno quieres tu conbatir?» «O nesçio», dixo el sandio, «e non sabes tu que ante debo saber que tengo en mi que non deva yr contra otro?» (138)

Zifar sleeps a short while and as the sun sets, still playing the fool, he passes through the lines of the besieging army without difficulty and enters the city where he will eventually marry the old King's daughter and become ruler of the city himself.

What can be the meaning of this strange episode which introduces Zifar into Mentón, the kingdom which he will eventually rule and shape into a *paradisus regnum*? He is a great knight who will soon vanquish singlehanded the attacking army of the King of Ester. Yet he is willing to play the part of a fool in order to gain entrance into the besieged city. I believe that the author conceived this section as a subfulfilment of those events in the life of Christ which showed the Son of the heavenly King as willing to humble himself to die on the cross in order to save mankind. The «guirnalda de fojas» would seem to parallel the crown of thorns placed upon the Saviour's head while the shouts of «Ahe aqui el rey de Menton» would recall the cries of «Hail, King of the Jews». The challenge which the innkeeper hurls at Zifar, «Well fool, defend your kingdom», predicts ironically what he will do just as the taunts of the soldiers at the foot of the cross stand as an absurd prelude to Christ's forthcoming victory over Satan. Zifar's reply to the innkeeper, «O nesçio... e non sabes tu que ante debo saber que tengo en mi que non deva yr contra otro...», is analogous to Jesus' explanation of His kingship before Pilate. «My kingdom is not of this world: if my kingdom were of this world, then would my servants fight, that I should not be delivered to the Jews: but now is my kingdom not from hence» (John 18.36).

Christ, by refusing to defend himself and thereby suffering death on the cross, makes possible salvation for the lost sons of Adam. Zifar undergoes humiliation and debasement in order to pass through the encircling lines of the army of Ester. He will soon sally forth from the city not as a fool but as a conquering hero who will put to flight those who mocked him.

The remarkable thing about this short vignette is the way in which the author catches the medieval impression of the inherent «meaning» in the experience of Christ. For the Middle Ages the most significant example which Jesus had left was that of His humility. If the Christian could follow in His humble footsteps, he would surely be saved. The author of the *Zifar* follows the *Flores de filosofia* in giving Luke 14.11 as the model which was to serve for Christ as well as for all His disciples. «Quien fuere umildoso sera ensalçado, e quien se quiere ensalçar sera abaxado» (295). The verse is a prediction of the action sequence by which Jesus will be humiliated by His death on the cross and then exalted by His victory in hell and His glorious Resurrection. Likewise all Christians should seek to adjust their lives to the same pattern. This is what the author of the *Zifar* has done with his hero outside the walls of Grades. He humbles the knight to the greatest possible degree as a preparation for his exaltation as the victor who will triumphantly re-enter the city after he has defeated the armies of the King of Ester (162). [50]

---

[50] This is the way in which Berceo presents the Crucifixion in the *Vida de Sancto Domingo de Silos:* «Mienbre vos como fizo el nuestro Redemptor, / que fue en cruz subido amuy grant desonor, / non quiso desçender maguer era Señor, / fasta rendio la alma quando El ovo savor» (ed. John D. Fitz-Gerald, Paris, 1904, 498).

When Zifar arrives in Mentón, and more particularly when he has vanquished the attacking enemy, the curse placed upon him through the misdeeds of the evil King Tarid is lifted. From the time that he leaves the hermit's hut for Mentón there is no more mention of his horses dying after ten days.

Zifar makes a redemptive journey during the Easter season which will not only improve his personal fortunes but also simultaneously elevate his decayed family line. While accomplishing this, he saves the widowed ruler of Galapia and the aged King of Mentón from aggresive neighbors. This literal, surface story of the knight and his family is exemplary in itself and the reader might have been expected to have benefited from the examples of virtue offered by them. At the same time, all that Zifar does, and even the way he does it, is reminiscent of events far more universal in their meaning and application.

First and foremost the reader would be reminded that Christ had undergone humiliation and degradation to be then resurrected in glory. Because of this Resurrection He made it possible for all men to experience a spiritual rebirth during this life (especially at Easter) and a resurrection of the body after death. The author has given a strong example of how this rebirth in the present life can occur by showing it to be present in the adventures of Zifar, who, in making his *transitus* from Tarta to Mentón, demonstrates that God's promise of deliverance concretized in Christ's actions can still be powerful and effective in the life of any Christian.

CHAPTER FIVE

MENTÓN—PARADISUS REGNUM

The end of Zifar's journey, the objective to which he moves from the shadows of Tarta, is the land of Mentón. The author of the *Zifar* envisioned Mentón as a land of peace and unity where men could live together in harmony. This harmony was in danger when Zifar first arrived in the country, not because of anything which the inhabitants had done nor because they had revolted against God or their ruler, but because their king no longer possessed the strength, so closely associated with the concept of the beard, which was necessary for their defense. Zifar, a knight sent by God to aid them, is more than capable of protecting the land of Mentón and deserves to rule a country whose very name implies potency. When Grima reaches Mentón after her nine-year sojourn in Orbín, she does not recognize her husband when she first sees him for «le avia cresçido mucho la barba» (177). Zifar's great beard symbolizes his capability of ruling his people well and of dealing with their enemies.[1]

The question of interest here is what the author of the *Zifar* is saying throughout the remainder of the first *exemplum* of the work. If we consider this portion in line with the ritual pattern, then events occurring after Zifar's *peripetia* in the hermit's hut constitute the theophany or period of joy. As Hardison says (285), both the pathos and theophany stages may be either very brief or extended to include a number of elements. The pathos

[1] One is, of course, reminded of the fisher king in the Old French Grail cycle who was usually presented as having a wound in the thighs. Because of this wound the fisher king lacked the capacity to rule his land as he once did. The implication was that the wound had affected his virility and consequently his ability to lead his people. Obviously the most effective symbols of male prowess would be the sexual organs and the beard.

period in the *Zifar* is quite long and contains a number of ideas
and references. The theophany begins as the knight moves
toward Mentón, continues with his freeing of the land from its
attackers, and goes on to his subsequent marriage to the daughter
of the former king. Grima then finds her way to Mentón as
do the sons. The family is united once more in a state of
happiness and power which sharply contrasts with their plight
in Tarta. [2] Even then the author does not end the theophany
period but continues it to include the revolt and punishment
of Count Nason. One would expect happenings in the *gaudium*
stage, the time of joy and fruition, to be even more significant
in their import for all men than the bleak trials of the pathos.
If Zifar's deeds prior to his *anagnorisis* and *peripetia* have meanings
applicable to the lives of other Christians, certainly his accomplish-
ments in his hour of fulfilment must also be viewed as symbolizing
possibilities attainable by the rest of mankind.

From the moment Zifar becomes king of Mentón the reader
is given a good demonstration of what the proper *modus operandi*
was for the medieval king who took his responsibilities seriously.
With Zifar as its ruler Mentón becomes the epitome of the
paradisus regnum in which every man receives justice as he deserves.
The knight was sent by God to be a saviour-emperor for the
people of Mentón who were suffering because their previous
ruler could no longer protect and serve the country. The old
and weak king of Mentón himself recognized Zifar as the answer
to his prayers and those of his people for salvation from the cruel
enemies who beset his land. «Cuydo que sea cavallero de Dios,
que nos ha aqui enbiado para nos defender e lidiar por nos»(153).
Doubtless the author was hoping that his reader would see
a parallel between Christ, the saviour-king dispatched by God
to see to the metaphysical needs of mankind, and Zifar, the
cavallero de Dios, who came to minister to God's people in an
earthly kingdom.

That Mentón is, indeed, a *paradisus regnum* is demonstrated
when Grima returns from Orbín. Her ship, guided by Christ
Himself, lands first in Ester, the country of the king who was

---

[2] The author of the *Zifar* is untroubled by the presence of Zifar's second wife,
the daughter of the former king of Mentón. After the Count Nasón episode she
dies (243) and there is no remaining obstacle to the reunion of the family in the
fullest sense.

vanquished by Zifar. She is warned by a good man whom she meets on the shore that it would be better for her not to remain in Ester but to go on to Mentón.

> E por mio acuerdo tu te yras morar a aquel regno de Menton, do ay un rey de virtud, que tenemos los omes que fue enbiado de Dios; ca mantiene su tierra en pas e en justicia, e es muy buen cavallero de sus armas e de buen entendimiento, e defiendese muy bien de aquellos quel quieren mal fazer. (169)

Grima does proceed to Mentón and finds that everything she has heard is true. The country is gaining such fame as a place to peacefully enjoy life in the pursuit of Christian virtue that people are migrating to it in great numbers from other less fortunate places. The inhabitants of Mentón have even become alarmed that their land may become too full. Grima realizes that there is space enough for all and draws a parallel between the good life in Mentón on this earth and that of the celestial paradise after the Day of Judgment.

> Por Dios, ome bueno, la bondat mas deve caber que la maldat, e la bondat largamente resçibe los omes e mantienelos en espaçio e en viçio, asy commo en el parayso las buenas almas; e la maldat resçibe los omes estrechamente e mantienelos en estrechura e en tormento, asy commo el infierno las almas de los malos. E porende devedes creer que la bondat deste regno segunt vos avedes aqui dicho, cabra todos los deste mundo s'y veniesen morar... (173-174)

The author of the *Zifar* sees Mentón, and likewise Roboán's kingdom of Triguida, [3] as exemplary for what life on this earth could be if men would only endeavour to live in peace and justice with one another. Mentón is in a certain sense the «terrestrial paradise» which fills out the formula Adam-Tarid and mankind-Zifar. Adam-Tarid lost Eden because of sin. Now whicheverman-Zifar has annulled the effect of this sin and has regained the primeval garden by fulfilling a quest suggested to him by God. The author of the *Zifar* is perhaps demonstrating here to his readers how life must be on this earth if man is to merit salvation after death.

During the Middle Ages there were two ways of looking at man's sojourn during this life; either as a necessary evil to be

---

[3] See *Zifar*, 515.

suffered and endured or as an equally necessary time of preparation, almost purification, of mankind for his life in the heavenly
kingdom. The idea that man could achieve a certain progress
during his earthly journey which would in some way foreshadow
the blissful state of the New Jerusalem was basic to Hebrew
prophetic literature [4] and had been picked up by such ecclesiastical authorities as Origen, Eusebius of Caesarea, St. John Chrysostom, St. Ambrose, and St. Jerome. Chrysostom's observation
that the Christian, with his homeland in heaven, should strive
to make the land of his pilgrimage something like the *patria*,
was typical of the attitude of many of the early writers in the
Church. [5]

St. Augustine, for various reasons, denied that any «true
progress» was to be found within the span of human history. [6]
The Bishop of Hippo did admit that certain good things were
possible within the realm of human experience on this earth, but
he was careful to point out that the Christian should never allow
his thoughts to wander from the forthcoming better things of
heaven. [7] Nowhere did he suggest that man would or could
achieve his final salvation in two stages, the first taking place
prior to the Judgment. [8] In fact, as Mommsen's study reveals,

[4] Cf. Stefan Porubcan's interpretation of Isaiah 54.10: «...the new covenant
of forgiveness and salvation will be performed and achieved in two stages. The
first one is spiritual and charismatic, we may call it 'soteriological', on the earth,
in the midst of human history, the purpose of which is to convert mankind from
its sins, by means of the gift of the spirit of God, into a righteous people, holy
to their God (very clear in Is. 44.3-5). Then comes the 'eschatological' stage, starting
from the cosmic transformation of the present world, by the way of some cataclysm,
into the world of the New Heaven and the New Earth...» (*Sin in the Old Testament,*
Rome, 1963, 545).
[5] See Ray C. Petry, *No Uncertain Sound: Sermons that Shaped the Pulpit Tradition* (Philadelphia, 1948), 70, for a translation of the sermon in which St. John Chrysostom makes this point.
[6] Theodore E. Mommsen, «St. Augustine and the Christian Idea of Progress»,
in *Medieval and Renaissance Studies,* ed. Eugene F. Rice (Ithaca, 1959), 197.
[7] St. Augustine makes this clear in the *City of God* when he discusses the
victory of Christians over evil: «Now, when victory remains with the party which
had the juster cause, who hesitates to congratulate the victor, and style it a necessary
peace? These things, are without doubt the gifts of God. But if they neglect
the better things of the heavenly city, which are secured by eternal victory and
peace never-ending, and so inordinately covet these present good things that they
believe them to be the only desirable things, or love them better than those things
which are believed to be better—if this be so, then it is necessary that misery follow
and ever increase» (trans. Marcus Dods, New York, 1950, xv, 4).
[8] This is in direct contrast to the traditions of Hebrew eschatological literature:
«...the new covenant of salvation is to be carried out gradually in two main stages.
The earlier stage... occurs on this earth, during human history; it is a period of

his purpose in *The City of God* was just the opposite. The metaphorical implications of St. Augustine's dualism of the cities did not really require a third term and he did not bother to provide one.

This «third term», despite the overwhelming influence of St. Augustine upon subsequent Christian thinking, continued to interest writers who viewed it, if not as strictly necessary for securing immortality, then at least as an aid to this end. Until the dissolution of the Empire, the *pax romana* had been conceived as the earthly counterpart of the heavenly kingdom, an idea which would be resurrected in the 13th century by Frederick II in regard to the Holy Roman Empire. [9] Probably through imitation of the Roman ideal, this same idea that a political entity on this earth could be a preparation for the afterlife came to be held for any kingdom and for any king. Jonas of Orleans suggests this in his writings to the future King Pepin when he discusses the kingdom that is wisely and competently ruled by a God-fearing sovereign. «Haec regni prosperitatem in praesenti faciunt, et regem ad coelestia regna meliora perducant... Saepe per regnum terrenum coeleste regnum proficit». [10] The famous 11th century Norman Anonymous definitely sees kings as a part of the redemptive machinery set in motion by Christ in order to save mankind. Through the royal *christi* the Kingdom of Heaven is to some extent brought about within the range of human history and the sublime conditions of the New Jerusalem are experienced by men while still in this life. [11]

charismatic and spiritual transformation, regeneration of mankind by means of the 'spirit of God'» (Porubcan, 546).

[9] II Thessalonians 2.1-8 implies that the Roman Empire will endure until the end of the world. Juan Manuel who of course describes the functioning of the perfect empire in the *Libro de los estados* has in mind the Holy Roman Empire which was considered to be the continuation of Rome's ancient dominion. See M. Torres López, «La idea del Imperio en el *Libro de los estados* de don Juan Manuel», *Cruz y Raya*, no. 2 (May 1933), 66.

[10] *PL, 106, 291.* Dora M. Bell points out that Jonas was implying that the king's mission had eschatological as well as immediate import: «Ainsi, grâce au roi, chaque membre du royaume pouvra aspirer à la réalisation de sa propre destinée et des grands buts de la vie humaine: la paix dans ce monde, le salut éternel dans l'autre» (*L'idéal éthique de la Royauté en France au moyen âge*, Geneva, 1962, 2).

[11] George H. Williams, *The Norman Anonymous of 1100 AD* (Cambridge, Mass., 1951), 15. The same idea is found in the *Siete Partidas:* «Ca en guardando bien estas cosas, viven derechamente, e con folgura e en paz, e aprovéchase cada uno de lo suyo, e a sabor de ello, e enriquecen las gentes, e amuchiguase el pueblo, e acrescientase el señorío, e refrenase la maldad, e crece el bien. E por todas estas razones dan carrera al ome, porque aya bien en este mundo e en el otro» (I, I, X).

Justice and peace were the two great social values of special responsibility to the ruler, for as long as these qualities were to be found, then there was no reason to fear disruptive strife. God placed the king over a land to insure that good government would exist for His people and to make sure that justice and peace would be maintained. Until the acceptance of Aristotelian views concerning the state in the 13th century, the king was viewed as the personal representative or even vicar of God in the land which he ruled. [12] As such he was personally responsible to God from Whom he had received the mandate for administering justice and for seeing that each man in the kingdom received his just due. [13] If God placed a just ruler over His people and if this ruler took his duty seriously, then the inhabitants of such a land would enjoy the benefits of an earthly peace and harmony, somewhat like that which was to reign in the heavenly city, which would allow them to prepare themselves in leisure for the afterlife.

The object of the quest of both Zifar and Roboán is to become such a ruler. The reason why they must carry out this *demanda* is that they have been granted certain qualities and virtues by God which are infrequently bestowed upon man. «... ca me semeja que Dios me quiere ayudar para yr adelante con ella; ca puso en mi, por la su merçed, algunas cosas señaladas de cavalleria que non puso en cavallero deste tienpo... E sy yo en esta demanda non fuese adelante, tengo que menguaria en los bienes que Dios en mi puso.» [14] Obviously certain individuals would possess the personal qualities or virtues which would more readily qualify them to be God's emissary. This superior individual, if he were made a king by God, would have to fulfil the aim of the theme of the *Zifar*, that is to return service for favor granted, by faithfully attempting to establish peace and justice in the land entrusted to him by God. If Zifar or his son should fail to undertake the quest suggested to them by the Almighty, they would lose the chivalric virtues given to them, and more important, they would not carry out Jesus' request evident in the parable of the talents in Matthew 25 and might find on the Day of Judgment that they did not merit salvation.

[12] See the *Siete Partidas*, I, VI, IV and Juan Manuel, *Libro del cavallero et del escudero*, 12.
[13] Cf. *Zifar*, 224.
[14] *Ibid.*, 33. The same can be seen as true for Roboán, 253.

To summarize, Zifar and Roboán, as a way of repaying God for the strength and virtues granted to them, set out on a quest which will lead them back to the terrestrial paradise from whence a sinful ancestor had been expelled. Within the literal context of the story this forebear was Tarid who lost his kingdom because of evil deeds, but the author clearly means to imply the loss of the Garden of Eden by Adam. He does not tell us that the establishment of exemplary kingdoms would be strictly necessary as a preparation for the Second Coming. It is only possible to argue that the message of redemption and the parallel between the actions of Christ and Zifar, so evident in the first section of the work would seem to suggest that this might have been the motive in the author's mind. Christ came to earth to wipe away the stain of the dark sin caused by Adam's disobedience. Once this was done the way was clear for the descendants of Adam to re-establish (or to approximate as much as possible) the conditions of the original Eden. This could only be done by obedience to the divine precepts apparent in God's word and by charity realized through the pursuit of virtue. It is true that immediately after Christ's death and Resurrection man had made little or no progress toward the setting up of a kingdom upon this earth which would resemble that Eden of long before. Nonetheless it was ever possible to do this, especially at that season of the year when the Church mystically recapitulates Christ's redeeming actions in the Easter liturgy.

An explanation of the manner in which the author of the *Zifar* seems to have envisioned the realization of this earthly kingdom is illustrated in a sermon by Isaac of Stella for the Feast of SS. Peter and Paul. Isaac asks a rhetorical question; «Why should men work and live together if this can lead to sin?» The answer is that man needs the mutual aid and protection afforded by the communal life. «... quia nondum sufficimus ad solitudinem, et, ut si ceciderit quis, habeat sublevantem se: item frater fratrem adjuvans, exaltabitur, sicut civitas munitas et fortis: denique quia bonum est et jucundum, habitare fratres in unum...»[15] Isaac ends his explanation with a reference to Psalm 132v where the communion of the saints in heaven and upon this earth is extolled and from where the author of the *Zifar* took the name

[15] *PL,* 194, 1860.

of Mentón. Isaac's point is that the common welfare of the individual cannot be maintained if he attempts to live in isolation. Only the collective pooling of talents can insure a state of well-being for all. This same conception is found in the *Zifar* although cast into the terms of the necessity of mutual defense rather than being presented as an idea of mutual service from one man to another. «... ca pues de un señorio son e de un logar, unos deven ser e de un coraçon en serviçio de su señor ên guardar e defender unos a otros, que non resçiban daño» (202-203). «... ca de derecho comunal e de egualdad es que son tenidos de anparar e defender a los unos e a los otros, tan bien las personas commo los algos, pues de una tierra e de un señorio son» (204). One might wish that the author of the *Zifar* had given this important social ideal in terms other than military aid and defense. He was, of course, writing a romance of chivalry and the usual business of the chivalry of the knight was the protection of the commonwealth. [16] It is then not surprising that the author illustrates this principle of unity in relation to the atmosphere of chivalric action which informs the work.

The key phrase in the presentation of this «bien comun» is «pues de una tierra e de un señorio son». Obviously it is possible for men to group themselves together into a society in which mutual aid and comfort is the primary aim. Once the principles of the natural body politic as envisioned by Aristotle had filtered down, medieval thinkers realized the existence of this body and began to write about it and explain it. Prior to the firm establishment of Peripatetic political philosophy, medieval man believed that an agent, sent by God, was necessary to give form and direction to human society. [17] This individual was in all cases the ruler or king, who, because he had been sent to occupy the same place in an earthly government that God holds in the heavenly realm, was capable of establishing, from his own hand so to speak, a commonwealth for the benefit of his subjects. The ruler was the incorporating principle who not only served

[16] I take the term «chivalry of the knight» from *Spain and the Western Tradition*, I, 98.
[17] «...the unity which they had was, on one hand, the unity of certain ideal forms which, by nature or supernatural grace, were common to all individual members; and, on the other hand, a unity of order achieved through the division of labor for the common good and the coordination of all activities to this end by the ruler» (Ewart Lewis, «Organic Tendencies in Medieval Thought», *APSR*, 32, 1938, 875).

as the symbol of unity for his people but also was strictly necessary if this unity were to exist.

> El rey es mayor sobre todo su regno por quien todos los del regno reciben dono de Dios en seer una cosa. Ca maguer ellos sean muchos, por derecha natura que el rey es uno, an todos ajuntarse a seer unos con el. [18]

It was the duty of the king, more than anything else, to look after the welfare of his subjects. The kingdom received the gift of unity the instant God placed the ruler over it. From that moment it depended largely upon the personal virtue and integrity of the overlord for its prosperity and well-being. If the king were strong, God-fearing and capable of defending the rights of his subjects, then the kind of terrestrial paradise discovered by Grima in Mentón would flourish. If the king were evil or weak, his land would fall prey to a plethora of sins and misfortunes.

The author of the *Zifar* conceived both Zifar and Roboán as archetypes of this God-given ruler through whom peace and justice could be poured out upon this earth. He not only presents their exemplary actions as a model for others, but also suggests the essential connection which exists between the ministrations of a just king to his people and those of Christ to all of humanity. Zifar and Roboán are able to complete their earthly missions because Christ accomplished certain deeds long ago and thereby prepared the way for them. Jesus came into the world and defeated Satan; because of His action man no longer remained under the bonds of original sin and the attainment of heaven was made possible. Zifar and Roboán free man from earthly demons such as Radan (destruction in Arabic) and establish earthly peace and harmony through which the kingdom of heaven is brought closer and made more appealing to humanity.

That the author of the *Zifar* did indeed envision Zifar and Roboán as the bestowers of Christian unity and fellowship upon

---

[18] Alfonso X, *Opúsculos legales,* I (Madrid, 1836), 13. Compare also «...por que el rey es cabeza e el regno cuerpo» (*Ibid.,* 30). The *Siete Partidas* has the same theme: «Et convino, que un home fuese Emperador, e hobiesse este poderio en tierra por muchas razones. La una, por toller desacuerdo de entre las gentes, e ayuntarlas en uno...» (II, I, I). The author of the *Zifar* follows the *Flores de filosofía* in viewing the king and his kingdom as two persons united by a kind of symbolic marriage into one body: «Ca el rey e su regno son dos personas, e asy commo una cosa ayuntada, dos en uno» (318).

their peoples is suggested by an over-riding image which goes hand in hand with the sermonic theme of the work. The great deed which Ferrand Martines accomplished and which serves to introduce the theme of the *Zifar* was the bringing of his lord Gonzalo Gudiel's body back to Toledo for burial. He thus fulfilled the promise which he had made and rendered service to Cardinal Gonzalo for all the great benefits which he had received. But the manner in which he returned service is most striking—he brought the Cardinal's body to its appointed resting place. If we consider the story of Ferrand Martines' great deed as an *exemplum*, and if we imagine the impression that such an undertaking might have made upon a medieval preacher always anxious for examples of great virtue with which to impress his listeners, we might be able to perceive more clearly what the author of the *Zifar* was hoping to demonstrate. I believe that he used the action of Ferrand Martines not only as an abstract illustration of *redde quod debes*, but also as a more direct example of what the individual who is king should do.

The modern imagination is not particularly challenged by what seems to be a rather macabre idea, the body of the Cardinal as the central image in the *exemplum*. For the Middle Ages with its great reverence for the relics of saints and its constant meditation upon the mystery of transubstantiation, such an image would have been viewed as a very powerful symbol. What might be taken as the typical medieval attitude toward such a figure is well illustrated in the prologue of the *Zifar* itself when Ferrand Martines describes the far from somber reception given to him when he reaches Spain with the body of Cardinal Gonzalo.

> E por do yvan salien le a resçebir todos los de las villas commo a cuerpo santo, con candelas en las manos e con ramos. E en las proçe-siones que fazien la clerezia e las ordenes, quando llegavan a las villas, non cantavan responsos de defuntos, synon «*ecçe saçerdos magnus*» e otros responsos e antifanas semejantes, asy commo a fiesta de cuerpo santo. (5) [19]

[19] This medieval attitude of joy and reverence toward the body of a holy man is also illustrated very well in the *Castigos e documentos* where the author describes the rewards which will accrue to holy and just men. These rewards are by no means only to be attained in the afterlife: «Por las santas obras bive el alma en parayso, e bive la su buena fama en el mundo, e el su cuerpo non podresçe, e faz Dios miraglos por los sus huessos e obedesçenlos rey e enperadores e perlados... fallaras que asi commo Jesu Cristo lo dixo, que asi se cunplio, que de los sus santos que resçibieron martirio por el, commo quier que por muchos martirios e por

The reaction of the Spanish people, both secular and clerical, is one of great joy that for the first time the body of a cardinal will rest in Spain. They do not look upon this body solely as the remains of a once living man but as a vessel which was joined to a pure and holy soul. The verse *ecce sacerdos magnus*, still used as the gradual in the Mass of a confessor bishop, suggests that the onlookers thought of Cardinal Gonzalo as a «confessor», a term which the *Catholic Encyclopedia* designates as applicable to men of «remarkable virtue and knowledge» who by the performance of great Christian deeds «began to be objects of veneration». [20]

It is clear that when the author of the *Zifar* refers to the processions and to «fiesta de cuerpo santo», he is comparing the celebrations in honor of the arrival of the body of Cardinal Gonzalo to those commonly accorded to the holy remains of a saint which a community might possess. The body of a saint held great power to work miracles and perform beneficial actions for believers as is demonstrated by the good wrought by the «cuerpo santo» of San Millan in Berceo's *Vida*. [21] The interesting point is that the body of a saint, preserved and prayed to by Christians, served a limited redemptive function similar on a restricted plane to that provided by Christ's body on the altar

muchas cuytas pasasen e a la çima las muertes que ovieron, non se perdieron los sus cabellos nin los sus huesos nin los sus cueros nin las sus carrnes, las quales son en reliquias por el mundo a loor e ha honrra de los preçiados e honrados e guardados» (ed. Agapito Rey, 176). The same attitude may be observed in Berceo's works. Cf. *Vida de Santo Domingo de Silos:* «El cuerpo glorioso, quando fue adovado» (529); «Metieron grant thesoro en muy grant angustura, / lucerna de grant lunbre en lenterna obscura» (531).

[20] Camillus Beccari, «Confessor», *CE,* 4, 215.
[21] Cf. 315. There are many examples throughout the *Vida de San Millán* and the *Vida de Santo Domingo de Silos* where the body of the saint preserved at the altar is revered and prayed to in much the same way that the Blessed Sacrament is: «Consintio el buen omne, non desvio en nada, / fizo el enclin luego, la bendiçion fue dada, / oro al Cuerpo Santo oraçion breviada, / dixo palabras pocas, razon bien acordada» *(Santo Domingo,* 98); «Entro al Cuerpo Santo fizo su oraçion» *(Ibid.,* 118). It was common for a community to take out in procession the body of any saint which it might possess, particularly if it were that of the patron of the place, in time of trouble or hardship or on the feast day of the saint. Cf. *Vida de San Millán,* «Aselmus so crïado, preciosa crïaçón, / con muchos buenos omnes de grant religïón, / aguisaron el cuerpo del precioso barón, / por darli sepultura e ferli procession» (312). See also José Amador de los Ríos, *Historia de la villa y corte de Madrid,* I (Madrid, 1860), 186. While it is technically true that the Roman ritual never included a feast in honor of the relics of a saint, cf. F. Chiovaro, «Relics», *NCE,* 12, 237, it would be but a small slip to call the feast day in honor of a saint «fiesta de cuerpo santo» if a community possessed some relic of the holy personage whom it was honoring and if the custom was to take this relic out in procession.

93

for the entire Christian community. The relics of a saint could aid in preserving those Christians who called upon the saint for succour. The body of Christ was given to man not only for earthly benefit but also for heavenly reasons as well. [22] It is impossible to say whether medievals perceived this relation between the «cuerpo santo» of a saint and the «cuerpo santo» of Christ on the altar, but the prologue of the *Zifar* would seem to imply that they did.

The divine mystery of Christ on the altar was linked throughout the Middle Ages with the idea of the body politic. Ernst Kantorowicz, in his work *The King's Two Bodies*, discusses the curious change of names which took place between the Host and the political organism. The Sacred Wafer which had originally been known as *corpus mysticum*, took, due to the influence of the dogma of transubstantiation, the name *corpus verum* which previously had been applied to the community of all Christians from St. Paul's dictum (I Cor. 12.14). [23] The commonwealth then assumed the title *corpus mysticum*. This was a logical development since it is much easier to envisage the «true» body of Christ as present on the altar each time Mass is celebrated than it is to visualize the entire Christian community as being there. But whether given a real or mystical interpretation, the Body of Christ on the altar and the body politic composed of all Christians must be viewed as the same thing. «Now ye are the body of Christ, and members in particular» (I Cor. 12,17). The only question involves how one relates the various terms of the metaphor.

Throughout the later Middle Ages the view was commonly held that the Host, the real and concrete example of Christ's body, given in communion to all faithful Christians, was the gift of God through which the human race could achieve its heavenly destination. Obviously this is a complicated idea. All mankind constitutes the Body of Christ, yet each person receives Christ's body in a finite sense at Communion. This *corpus verum* must

---

[22] The Body of Christ was known as «cuerpo santo» in the Middle Ages. The procession of the Blessed Sacrament at Rouen Cathedral on Palm Sunday, which survived down until the end of the 18th century, was called the Corps-Saint procession (Edmund Bishop, *Liturgica Historica,* Oxford, 1918, 276-278). A villancico lauds Baby Jesus in the manger with the term «cuerpo de santo» (Richard B. Donovan, *The Liturgical Drama in Medieval Spain,* Toronto, 1958, 37-38, 186).
[23] Ernst Kantorowicz, *The King's Two Bodies* (Princeton, 1957), 206.

represent an individualization in human terms which aids the Christian in maintaining himself as a part of the metaphysical whole, the *corpus mysticum*. Because of the Sacrifice of the altar man was able to leave this vale of sin and set out toward his heavenly destination. This was the principal viewpoint and concern of the Corpus Christi plays of medieval England which emphasized the Sacrament's power to effect a change in the human condition. [24] In Spain the same ideas were prevalent concerning the efficacy of Christ's great gift to mankind. [25] The 15th-century *Flos Sanctorum* of Pedro de la Vega reflects this thinking as well as underlining another widely held concept having to do with the ultimate destiny of humanity. For Pedro de la Vega the Body of Christ on the altar was that which effectively incorporated all Christians into the mystical Body of Christ.

> Y por la virtud deste santo sacramento somos hechos todos los fieles una cosa, conviene saber miembros con nuestro señor Jesu Christo y un cuerpo con el, segun lo enseña el apostol Sant Pablo a donde dize. Todos somos un cuerpo de Jesu Christo, y somos hechos sus miembros. Por que todos los que son baptizados son encorporados en nuestro señor Jesu Christo por el baptismo y son hechos sus miembros y esta encorporacion es figurada, y esforçada y conservada por la virtud deste santissimo sacramento. [26]

The king is the active agent granted by God who by his virtue and great deeds imposes earthly political unity upon his people.

[24] As V. Kolve points out: «...instead of concentrating on the Sacrament's temporal power to work miracles, to convince and convert, it looked instead on its eternal power to alter the destiny of the human race... Except for this sacrifice and gift, even the good would have been damned guilty of Adam's sin» (*The Play Called Corpus Christi,* Stanford, Calif., 1966, 48).

[25] Since the most likely date for the *Zifar* is 1301 (cf. Erasmo Buceta, «Algunas notas históricas al prólogo del *Cavallero Cifar*», RFE, 17, 1930, 18-36), it is almost impossible to state with any certainty that the Feast of Corpus Christi could have been known and celebrated in Spain at the time of its composition. Pope Urban IV established this Festival in 1264 but Dom Gregory Dix states that the majority of Italian churches had not yet adopted it fifty years later (*The Shape of the Liturgy,* Westminster, 1945, 586). It is possible that Corpus Christi was celebrated in Toledo as early as 1280 (cf. F. G. Very, *The Spanish Corpus Christi Procession,* Valencia, 1962, 4), thus the author of the *Zifar* who very likely was a cleric in the imperial city might have been familiar with the Feast. At any rate the belief in the efficacy of the Body of Christ on the altar far predated the establishment of Corpus Christi and was, in fact, the reason for the special day in the first place.

[26] (Seville, 1568) cxxvi. Alfonso X's *Setenario* stresses the good life which the Christian will enjoy in this world because of the effects of the Sacrament of the altar: «...otrossí Nuestro Ssennor Ihesu Cristo da conplidamente buen govyerno en este mundo e mantiénel en el otro al que el ssu cuerpo rreçibe...» (ed. Kenneth Vanderford, Buenos Aires, 1945, 158).

But the factor which makes this oneness possible in a real and metaphysical sense and which even serves as a model, is Christ's true body on the altar, the earthly entity which symbolizes the mystical body to which all Christians will be assimilated after the Second Coming. God has given to His people the sacrifice of the altar through which they may attain the heavenly kingdom. He, at the same time, gives to them a king to guide them and to protect them and thereby make sure that their earthly habitation will be a fit preparation for their heavenly one.

Because of the great gift of the Body of Christ on the altar which makes salvation possible, and in line with the medieval idea of *redde quod debes*, man should be not only grateful to God for this gift but should also seek to return something to Him in appreciation for it. The Mass itself poses this idea in the form of a rhetorical question during the Celebrant's Communion as is demonstrated in the translation and explanation of the Mass given in the *Setenario*. «¿Qué daré al Ssennor por todas las cosas que me dió? Cáliçe de ssalvamiento rreçibré, e llamaré al Ssennor; e sseré ssalvo de mis enemigos.» [27] The St. Andrew Missal explains that at this point in the Mass there is «In the soul of the celebrant as in that of every faithful Christian who communicates... a predominate feeling of thanksgiving» (835). Thanksgiving is the modern view of what this phase of the Mass means, but medieval man, upon hearing the question «What shall I give?» would doubtless have answered in more concrete terms. His reply would probably have reflected the full significance of *redde quod debes* and would have committed the Christian to definite deeds in repayment for Christ's great gift. Obviously the human offering would have been hopelessly inferior to the divine one. This was of no consequence as long as that which each man offered was the best that he could.

The responsibility of that man who had been made king by the hand of God was far greater than that of the average Christian and his duty was completely clear. In return for the great dignity and honor which had been given him, he was to return service to God by governing his people well so that it might be easier for them to prepare themselves for the kingdom of

[27] *Ibid.*, 242. The Latin words of the Mass read as follows: «Quid retribuam Domino pro omnibus quae retribuit mihi? Calicem salutaris accipiam, et nomen Domini invocabo. Laudens invocabo Dominum, et ab inimicis meis salvus ero.»

heaven. Thus the king, if he partook of the divine gift of the Body of Christ as an aid to his soul's health, could only merit the benefit possible from this communion if he recognized his responsibilities toward the earthly *corpus politicum* which had been entrusted to his care.

Ferrand Martines fulfilled his obligation to his benefactor and at the same time brought the body of a holy man to rest in the city of Toledo. He observed *redde quod debes* as completely as he could. If one applies the absolute surface meaning of the *exemplum* in the prologue to the romance as a whole, it would imply that Zifar and Roboán should render service to God their benefactor just as Ferrand Martines did to his. But the image of the «cuerpo» looms too powerful in the *exemplum* to have been of only incidental importance. Its symbolism must carry over also into the meaning of the romance as a whole.

The author of the *Zifar* following the *Flores de filosofia* says that the king must fear God and love «merced e mesura» more than anyone else because «Dios le fizo merçed e le dio regno que mantoviese, e metio en su poder cuerpos e averes del su pueblo» (318). It is the obligation of the king to ensure the physical well-being of his subjects while they are on this earth. Further along in the *Castigos* section the author uses excerpts from the *Flores* to illustrate the importance of *seso*. «Onde sabet que el cuerpo es commo el regno, e el seso commo el rey, e las maneras commo el pueblo; pues sy podiere el rey mas quel pueblo, endresçarlo-ha, e sy podiere el pueblo mas quel rey, puede se perder el rey e el pueblo» (341). The king, the *seso*, is responsible for the welfare of the kingdom and people, *cuerpo y maneras*. If he fails in his duty, all three are lost—not only in this world but also for the next. «E sabet quel seso es guiador del cuerpo en este mundo e del alma en el otro»; the author of the *Zifar* implies that the king's solicitude for his kingdom, the *cuerpo*, is of great importance in aiding both him and his people to reach heaven.

It is likely that the outstanding image of the *exemplum* in the prologue, the translation of the body, is also conveyed to the adventures of Zifar and Roboán. Both, in order to fulfil the requisites of *redde quod debes*, must preserve and secure the *cuerpo*, the kingdom, entrusted to their care. They have the same responsibility for the *corpus politicum* under their tutelage that Ferrand

97

Martines had for the body of Cardinal Gonzalo; they must do all that they can to see that their souls and the souls of their people reach the eternal destination provided for them by God.

The author of the *Zifar* presents an extraordinary metaphor, that of the body of the Cardinal suggesting the body politic, as the dominant image of his work. It is an image which, if properly interpreted, could not have failed to impress any royal reader who might have happened upon the work. The juxtaposition of the deeds of Ferrand Martines on one plane against those of Zifar and Roboán on another should have given a clear example of how each man, but particularly the king, must do his proper duty in this life if he is to fulfil what is expected of him by God and if he is to merit the saving grace of Jesus Christ.

If the author of the *Zifar* did indeed intend that the king should play a role in the eschatological destiny of his people, then the question arises concerning how the ruler should function in regard to the Church which, of course, possessed direct control over the necessary sacraments. Since, according to the teachings of St. Paul, all Christians constitute one Body of Christ, it follows that one ruler should have ultimate authority and ultimate responsibility to God for this Body. Christ had given the keys of the kingdom to St. Peter, the spiritual authority, while urging his followers to render unto Caesar the things which are Caesar's (Luke 20.25). The consequent problem as to which of the two established powers, the ecclesiastical or the secular, should be dominant was not an easy one to resolve.

Pope Gelasius (d. 497) gave a solution which was to be constantly challenged throughout the Middle Ages by one side or the other, but which was basically the only solution if Church and state were to co-exist. [28] Each of these bodies would be considered as a distinct authority in its own right without visible superior in its own realm. The state would have full dominion in matters of civil administration while the Church would exercise control in spiritual matters. Charlemagne upset this delicate balance by placing the Empire once more within the confines of the Church. [29] This is not to say that he surrendered

[28] *Epistola,* VIII, *PL,* 59, 42.
[29] From the time of Charlemagne «Empires and kingdoms were *in* the Church, not *beside* the Church, as in St. Augustine and Gelasius, and not *above* the Church, as in the caesaro-papism of the Byzantine Empire» (Gerhart B. Ladner, «Aspects of Mediaeval Thought on Church and State», *RP,* 9, 1947, 408).

power to Rome. Rather he conceived himself as a king or ecclesiastical emperor who could hold sway in clerical and secular matters. The dispute concerning whether one of the «two swords» [30] should predominate continued throughout the period of the Investiture struggles up until the time of Frederick II who created a purely secular state «which, while free from the spiritual authority of the Church, should present a complete whole vitalised by spiritual forces». [31] The Church did not tarry in challenging such an affront to its power. The quarrel flared up again between Philip the Fair of France and Pope Boniface VIII who in his Bull *Unam Sanctam* declared once more that any king or emperor was of necessity «vassal du Saint-Siège». [32]

Despite these tensions between the secular and ecclesiastical authorities, for most of the Middle Ages Church and state managed to function fairly well as a co-ordinate whole. While the Church might never admit that a temporal ruler could in any way be the equal of a spiritual one, who controlled the ultimate and eternal destiny of man, actual Church policy tended to follow along constructive lines which carried out Christ's exhortation in regard to the rights of the secular ruler. [33]

This is the attitude of the author of the *Zifar* which is clearly expressed in the *Castigos* section of the work. He recognizes that the Pope is superior in things spiritual (270) while at the same time realizing that, practically speaking, the spiritual head must not interfere with the temporal power if an equilibrium is to be maintained.

> E el rey deve tener para castigar espada e cochiello material, e el saçerdote espada o cuchiello espritual, e el rey es dicho rey de los cuerpos, e el saçerdote de las almas; ca el uno syn el otro non pueden bien conplir su ofiçio, nin puede ser que el uno aya estos dos ofiçios, que sea rey de los cuerpos e rey de las almas. (312-313)

If the two authorities do learn and accept a *modus vivendi* such as this, the hearts of men will be united in one and the benefits

---

[30] The idea of the «two swords» which originated with Pope Gelasius became widespread. Examples of its use may be seen in St. John Chrysostom, Homily 4 on Isaiah 6.1, *PG*, 56, 125 and in St. Thomas Aquinas, *De regimini principum*, 3, 10.

[31] Ernst Kantorowicz, *Frederick the Second*, trans. E. D. Lorimer (New York, 1957), 229.

[32] Robert Folz, *L'Idée d'empire en occident du Vᵉ au XIVᵉ siècle* (Paris, 1953), 155.

[33] See Anton-Hermann Chroust, «The Corporate Idea and the Body Politic in the Middle Ages», *RP*, 9 (1947), 435.

8

expected of the well-functioning *bien común* will result. King and priests and people must all subscribe to «una ley» which can be realized if the king will seek advice from the Church. «... e el rey deve demandar consejo al saçerdote, ca es lunbre e regla en estas cosas, e conviene que el rey faga onrra al saçerdote asy commo a padre e que le aya asy commo a corretor del e del pueblo e quel ame asy commo a guardador de la fe» (313).

The author of the *Zifar*, who himself may have been a churchman, thus advocates that the temporal ruler should exercise direct power over the *bien común* guided by the counsel of the Church. It is notable that throughout the work neither Zifar nor Roboán ever seems to seek this advice. On the other hand they do faithfully attend Mass at every opportunity. It might be inferred that the author of the *Zifar* preferred to envision a more direct communication between God and the king facilitated by prayer and eucharistic communion. The king would, in and of himself, be made aware of the will of God and could then seek to follow it as best he might.

The author of the *Zifar* does not end his first major *exemplum* as would be expected after the knight and his family are reunited in the peace and prosperity of Mentón; rather he extends it through another lengthy episode which deals with the treason and revolt of Count Nason. As this section terminates the theophany phase of the ritual pattern, it is strange to find it treating a subject so foreign to the atmosphere of Christian harmony which Zifar has established in Mentón. This revolt of Count Nason is a parallel in the first *exemplum* to the uprising of the kings of Garba and Safira and the seven counts against Roboán in the last *exemplum*. In each case father and son are respectively forced to deal with a fierce rebellion, perpetrated by sworn vassals, before they can consolidate firm rule over their kingdoms.

The author of the *Zifar* has introduced these revolts as examples because they are demonstrative of the exact opposite of the fulfilment of the theme *redde quod debes*. The traitor, instead of returning service and loyalty to his benefactor for the boons which he has received, does the reverse.

> ... ca los omes de buena sangre e de buen entendimiento, quanto mas dizen dellos loando las sus buenas costunbres e los sus buenos fechos, tanto mas se esfuerçan a fazer lo mejor con umildat; e los de vil logar e mal acostunbrados, quanto mas los loan sy algunt

bien por aventura fazen, tanto mas orgullesçen con sobervia, non queriendo nin gradesçiendo a Dios la virtud que les faze... (190)

Treason against one's earthly lord is such a serious crime because it represents in terms of this world what Satan's insurrection had meant in heaven.

The archetype for rebellion and treason throughout time was the revolt of Lucifer and his angels which resulted in their being cast down into hell. All examples of disloyalty, disruption, and disaffection in this world refer back to that primordial cataclysm when excessive pride led to downfall. Adam's disobedience in the Garden of Eden and his subsequent loss of innocence was man's first bitter experience in a series of awful events, modeled upon Lucifer's descent, which would not end until the final victory of the Lamb over Babylon as foretold in Revelation 17. That medievals believed the influence of these archetypal happenings to be continually present in history is very well exemplified in such works as John Lydgate's *The Siege of Thebes* where the destruction of the city is actually said to have begun with Lucifer's pride and revolt in heaven, the exemplar for all war and destruction on earth. [34]

Since the king was the vicar of God in the administration of the secular realm, any revolt against him indirectly was a sign of disloyalty toward the Almighty. For this reason the author of the *Zifar*, following thinking promulgated at the court of Alfonso X, portrays the traitor as even worse than the man who has committed sacrilege. [35] The sinner who has rebelled against God and is excommunicated has endangered only his own soul. The traitor not only perjures himself before the Almighty by the breaking of his oath of fealty, he also places the entire human commonwealth into jeopardy by not serving the overlord whom God had chosen to guide and unify His people. [36]

One of the metaphors chosen by the author of the *Zifar* to illustrate the evils of treason is striking in the way it relates to the overlying image of the well-guided, well-protected body politic. Treason, says the author, is like leprosy. «Onde sy

---

[34] Robert W. Ayers, «Medieval History, Moral Purpose, and the Structure of Lydgate's *Siege of Thebes*», *PMLA*, 73 (1958), 467.
[35] See Angel Ferrari Núñez, «La secularización de la teoría del Estado en las 'Partidas'», *AHDE*, 11 (1934), 447-456.
[36] Cf. *Zifar*, 222.

los omes quesieren parar mientes a saber que cosa es trayçion, fuyrian della commo de gafedat...» (222). Although the comparison is not directly stated, the reader senses immediately the parallel which seems to be implied between the effect of leprosy upon the human body and that of treason upon the *corpus mysticum* guided by the king. Treason is the moral equivalent to leprosy in that the ravages which this disease effects upon a real body can be metaphorically viewed as the destruction of a commonwealth by those who dismiss their loyalty and revolt against their ruler.

The Count Nason episode as an example of treason is not allegorical in the *quid pro quo* sense unless we consider its last section in which el Caballero Atrevido enters the mysterious lake where the executed Nason's ashes have been thrown. The kingdom which the knight finds there ruled by a fiendish woman and filled with plants and animals which reach maturity after only seven days must be suggestive of something beyond what appears on the literal plane. [37] As explained in Chapter Eight, the story of Roboán's struggle with his vassals appears to be a «poetic allegory» in that it is a posing of the virtuous knight against personifications of certain variations of the Seven Deadly Sins. But these adventures of both father and son are in a wider sense «subfulfilments» which demonstrate the continuation of the pattern of disruption established at the beginning of time. Lucifer's treason will continue to make itself felt in the lives of men until the Second Coming finally isolates God's people from all evil.

By giving us positive and negative approaches to *redde quod debes* the author of the *Zifar* formulates an almost dialectic treatment of his theme. The typological patterns of good set forth by the actions of holy men were not the only ones to influence the behaviour of history. Evil examples also existed which would constantly find expression in the lives of those who elected to follow Satan rather than Jesus. In earthly terms the extension of the theophany section in the first *exemplum* to cover Count Nason's revolt is a reminder to the reader that the procuring of peace and prosperity within history could not be an easy venture. Men of virtue, those always ready to follow the precepts implied by *redde quod debes*, would have to be

---

[37] See Chapter Three.

constantly prepared to struggle against those wishing to violate its principles. The victories of Zifar and Roboán in their conflicts with the rebellious vassals suggest on the eschatological plane the final triumph of Christ over all the legions of the Devil at the end of time. Just as Roboán's marriage to Seringa points to certain events foreordained for the period of the Second Coming so the battles of father and son foreshadow that final confrontation with evil.

In the first of the three major exempla of the *Zifar*, the author unfolds a drama concerned with the redemption and purification of man. The action of the knight Zifar in leaving the darkness and unhappiness of Tarta in order to reach the felicity of Mentón is illustrative of not just one man's personal victory over Satan; it is to be taken as that of all men collectively. At the same time Zifar is an individual and the author can make use of his individuality to show how any man, particularly one blessed with strength and virtue, can rise to a position of great importance.

The office most concerned with the daily welfare of all humanity was that of the king who was granted the temporal sword by God. If it could be insured that a virtuous man, one ever conscious of his duty toward God while mindful of his earthly responsibilities, would hold that position, then the commonwealth would prosper and its citizenry could prepare itself in peace and harmony for their heavenly destination. Of course it is implicit in the *Zifar* that only God Himself is capable of choosing the ruler who could accomplish so much. At the same time it is clear that the individual who is endowed with the characteristics necessary for such leadership should always endeavor to be ready to accept and carry out this responsibility were it to be entrusted to him.

CHAPTER SIX

THE MIRROR OF PRINCES

The inclusion of a major *exemplum* modeled upon the *de regimine principum* was not accident on the part of the author of the *Zifar*. It is likely that this section provides the key needed for understanding how the other two *exempla*, in the broadest sense, portray the meaning of the sermonic theme. The «mirror of princes», a genre of great vogue and importance in the Middle Ages, was conceived primarily as a means of education for future rulers. But it also served both as a safe means for the philosopher to offer advice to the throne and as a repository for systems of thought and points of view which otherwise might have been ignored. The «Castigos del rey de Mentón» represents the ideas of the author of the *Zifar* concerning kingship and government and the place of the ruler within the divine order.

The section begins with the basic theme of the entire work *redde quod debes* cast into new form. «Mios fijos cosa muy verdadera es que cualquier bien e don perfecto que en nos es, que del omnipotente Dios lo recebimos. [James 1.17] ... y pues tanta obligacion le tenemos, que todo bien del rescebimos todo nuestro amor en el pongamos» (255). In the next two lines the author of the *Zifar* equates this «don perfecto» with the ability to save himself and to protect himself from evil. The way to maintain these gifts and to further develop them is to fear God «... Ca dize en Santa Escriptura que el comienço de la sabiduria es el temor de Dios...» [Psalm 111.10 and Proverbs 1.7 and 9.10] and to always follow «buen consejo» leaving «mal consejo» aside. As an example of those who prefer «mal consejo» to «buen consejo» the author of the *Zifar* presents in *exemplum* style the story of a young king of Armenia who encounters a preacher beside the road exhorting passers-by to lead a better life. The young king tells the preacher that he must abbreviate his message for him since he cannot detain himself long to listen to moral precepts. The preacher replies that it is absurd to wish to have the works of God summed up in a few words.

> Los fechos de Dios son tantos e de tantas maneras que se non pueden dezir en pocas palabras, mayormente a aquellos que tienen oio por las vanidades deste mundo mas que por castigos e las palabras de Dios... e dexat oyr la predicaçion a aquellos que han sabor de la oyr e se pagan de conosçer la merçed que les Dios fizo en les dar entendimiento para las oyr e las aprender... (256)

The author of the *Zifar* has said that man receives «razon e entendimiento» as a gift from God. But in order to merit having «entendimiento» and in order for this faculty to be useful, he must develop it. This development is graphically given here in terms of hearing and following «buen consejo» delivered by a preacher. The importance of this brief *exemplum* is that it implies the medieval conception of the relation of learning to salvation.

In the parable of the sowers in Mark 4 Christ says that certain men are capable of receiving and understanding the message of salvation while others are not. Jesus further declares that the mysteries of the Christian faith may be comprehended eventually by those capable if only they will endeavor to make themselves ready. «For there is nothing hid, which shall not be manifested; neither was anything kept secret, but that it should come abroad. If any man have ears to hear, let him hear» (Mark 4.22-23). This and similar texts (Matthew 10.26 for example) meant to the Middle Ages exactly what the author of the *Zifar* was saying at the beginning of the *Castigos* section; that is, that the man who has the intellectual ability to find the road to salvation must do so. The preacher at the roadside beckoning to the passing young king is in effect making it possible for him to follow the biblical admonition «If any man have ears to hear, let him hear».

Speech and hearing were of such importance to medieval man because the divine wisdom of God prior to the Incarnation had been characterized in verbal terms as *logos*, the Word. Under the New Dispensation this Logos would manifest itself to believers through words and word groupings. Christians had from the

time of St. Augustine looked upon language, particularly erudite
language, as the unique human means of communication with
the spiritual realms of the divine.[1] Through the mode of
language man could learn about the mysteries of God as they
were presented in the world around him and by apprehending
these mysteries he could place himself on the right road to
salvation. Of the five senses only two, speech and hearing,
were to be any benefit to the Christian in his pilgrim's journey
through this world toward the celestial homeland.[2] Language,
filled with meaning by the fact that God had seen fit to humanize
His divine wisdom, the *logos*, in Jesus Christ, became the most
important aspect of the «New Law» as differentiated from the
old code of Moses. The fact that words in the Canon of the
Mass were used by the priest to convert bread and wine into the
True Body of Christ continued and augmented the reverence for
verbal expression which the medieval imagination had first felt
because of its awe for the divine *logos*.[3]

We have seen in Chapter Two that medieval man felt that
God had manifested Himself to mankind in the Bible and in the
multitudinous facets of His physical world. Not only was there

[1] Marcia Colish, *The Mirror of Language* (New Haven, 1968), points out that
this was a commonplace among medieval thinkers: «They all (Augustine, Anselm,
St. Thomas) hold that human powers of speech and conceptualization are capable
of signifying Divine truths accurately although incompletely. They also maintain
that human words may turn the non-believer in the direction of God or help a
believer to deepen his understanding of what he believes...» (316). The *Primera
crónica general* in the section where it treats the origin of writing implied how the
medieval considered human speech as the basis of reason. It was, of course, through
reason that man was able to approach God: «...fallaron las figuras de las letras;
et ayuntando las fizieron dellas sillabas, et de sillabas ayuntadas fizieron dellas partes; e ayuntando otrossi las partes, fizieron razon, et por la razon que viniessen
a entender los saberes et se sopiessen ayudar dellos...» (ed. Ramón Menéndez Pidal,
Madrid, 1955, I, 3).
[2] As Juan Manuel says: «Et todo lo que se puede fazer de las cosas spirituales
non alcança[n] a ello todos los sesos corporales, ca la cosa spiritual non se puede
veer con los spirituales nin se puede palpar nin se puede oler. Mas para ende se
oyr, et de lo [que] omne ende oye puede depués fablar en ello. Et asý de los çinco
sesos corporales, et los que son oýr et fablar alcançan algo de las cosas spirituales,
et lo que estos dos sesos alcançan judga y entiende depués la razón natural el entendimiento, et por el entendimiento del omne que non es letrado, non puede judgar
tan complidamente commo era mester en las cosas spirituales...» (*Libro del cavallero
et del escudero*, in *Obras de don Juan Manuel*, I, 28).
[3] See Walter Ong, «Wit and Mystery», *Spec*, 22 (1947), 317. Juan Manuel
also clearly expresses this idea: «...pero según el mi flaco saber, tengo que el más
alto estado es el clérigo missacantano, por que en éste puso Dios tamanno poder,
que por virtud de las palabras que él dize, torna la hostia, que es pan, en ver-
dadero cuerpo de Jesucristo, et el vino, en su sangre verdadera...» (*Libro del cavallero et del escudero*, 13).

present in Holy Scripture and in the universe the reflections of the divine in a passive sense, but there also existed the evidence of that heavenly economy which had governed history from the Creation and which would continue to hold sway until the Second Coming. Man could find and read the outline of this plan if he knew how to look for it and if he could interpret it once he had found it. Language, particularly in the sense that it had been redeemed along with the rest of creation by the death and Resurrection of Christ, was the Christian's only tool in that it and it alone could lead to that wisdom which would allow him to interpret God's signs correctly. [4]

The author of the *Zifar* says that the most basic gift of God is «buen seso natural» (297), the inborn ability to learn. If man then builds upon this foundation through study facilitated by the mode of language, he eventually will possess wisdom which is the key to «entendimiento» the highest of values. «E todos los omes de buen seso pueden llegar a grant estado, mayormente seyendo letrados, e aprendiendo buenas costunbres; ca en la letradura puede ome saber quales son las cosas que deve usar e quales son de las que se deve guardar» (298). These two things, «seso» and «letradura», are of consummate importance to the human race because they «mantienen el mundo en justicia e en verdat e en caridat» (298).

The sermonic theme given at the beginning of the *Zifar* implies that «buen entendimiento» is the gift of God for which man most owes service (6). An important point which the author would have to clarify in regard to this idea of «buen entendimiento» as the most important boon is just how man might return something to God in line with the principle *redde quod debes* for that which he had received. The *Castigos* section is precisely the illustration in action of this point. It demonstrates the way in which the Christian, in particular the king, can repay God for his «don perfecto» of «entendimiento». He can render service indirectly by passing on, through the inspired mode of redeemed speech, those ideas and precepts which he himself, guided by God, has found to be valuable in aiding mankind to achieve salvation. He can be the intermediary teacher necessary to convey and interpret the divinely stimulated wisdom which

---

[4] See Colish, 244.

man has painstakingly eked out, recorded, and remembered by means of words. [5] God, through the death and Resurrection of Jesus Christ, has given to men the opportunity for redemption. Heavy in the *Zifar*, however, and in other medieval works is the implication that the human race must take an active part in the process of salvation by striving to re-establish upon the earth the delightful conditions forfeited by Adam. This restoration of the vanished Eden can be facilitated by the slow accretion of knowledge and experience in the human community. The father must pass on to the son all that he has learned. At the same time «He who has ears, let him hear». The young man, granted «buen seso» by God, had an equal obligation to pay attention to the teachings of the older man who had himself in his youth used his natural gifts in conjunction with «buen consejo» and «letradura» to achieve wisdom. The short *exemplum* of the preacher and the young king given by Zifar to his sons at the beginning of the *Castigos* presents in another fashion the same message as the longer section. Both are examples in miniature implying the process by means of which master and pupil, preacher and listener, can facilitate the slow redemptive evolution of mankind. [6]

The *de regimine principum* furnishes the natural model for the author of the *Zifar* to follow in his illustration of how learning can be utilized for the benefit of mankind. Since the king was of such crucial importance in creating an atmosphere of peace

---

[5] «Virtually all of the basic treatises such as Thomas Aquinas' *Governance of Princes,* Durand of Mende's handbook on liturgical symbolics, Vincent de Beauvais's *Mirror of History,* and Humbert of Romans' book *On the Education of Preachers,* have one common concern. The teachers of Christ's Church on earth have their commission from heaven to inculcate in human society the associational principles of celestial community» (Ray C. Petry, *Christian Eschatology and Social Thought,* New York and Nashville, 1956, 374). Isaiah 54.13 hints that the education of children is important as a step toward the achievement of peace and justice on the earth: «And all the children shall be taught of the Lord; and great shall be the peace of thy children...» Marcia Colish (179) points out that both St. Augustine and St. Thomas Aquinas believed that God used the teacher as an instrument toward the realization of His kingdom.

[6] Robert Kaske demonstrates the importance which preaching held for the Middle Ages when he says that «...the final triumph of the *predicatio Ecclesiae* (embracing both instruction in truth and admonishment to good) is almost as prominent a feature of the final time as is the advent of Christ. A popular text is Matt. 24.14, with its apparent prophecy that the end will come only after the Gospel has been preached in all parts of the world» («Dante's 'DXV' and 'Veltro'», *Trad,* 17, 1961, 245). Thus the preaching and acceptance of the things of God was fully necessary to prepare the world for the Second Coming of Christ. The *Castigos* is a graphic presentation of how this «preaching» and «teaching» can take place.

and justice in the land under his governance, it was necessary that he especially be aware of his debt to God and of his obligation to fulfil it by ruling well. Young princes could gain an insight into their duties either from the available works of the *de regimine principum* genre or by following the advice of wise counselors such as prelates of the Church who were knowledgeable in the ways of man and of God. [7] The author of the *Zifar* effectively implies both of these by beginning his *Castigos* section, evocative of the «mirror of princes» in form and substance, with the *exemplum* of the young king and the preacher. He is saying to his readers that these are the two ways by which princes may be prepared for the important task which is their duty.

The over-all implication of the *Castigos* section is that man, exemplified in the prince, can create for himself an environment of peace and harmony by the slow accretion of knowledge from generation to generation. [8] This can be accomplished because the diligent king who develops his God-given «buen seso natural» through «letradura» and «buen consejo» will become wise and will naturally seek to establish justice and happiness throughout his realm.

The author of the *Zifar* has conceived the *Castigos* as the second of his major *exempla*. Since we read the work in linear fashion and since its events take place in historical sequence, we would expect that the gradual evolution of the author's plan, that which he is trying to say about the theme *redde quod debes*, would unfold itself step-by-step as we proceed through the book. The second major *exemplum* would then have to depend upon the first major *exemplum* for meaning in the same way that it relies upon it in regard to context in time and place. «Los hechos de Roboán» would continue the author's vision and give fulfilment to the ideas and conceptions originated and commented upon in the first two *exempla*.

The previous two chapters have attempted to demonstrate that the first major *exemplum* of the book, the «Cavallero de Dios y Rey de Mentón» deals basically with the curing by man, with the death and Resurrection of Christ as the enabling factor, of the earthly ills resulting from the Fall of Adam. The knight Zifar through his penitential and redemptive actions returns

---

[7]   As the author of the *Zifar* recommends on 313.
[8]   See Chapter 146 and 148 and p. 379 of the *Castigos*.

mankind figurally to the gate of the earthly paradise. In the second *exemplum* the author creates a static situation which probably alludes to the period when man will slowly raise himself through learning. In the third section Zifar's son completes the process so that man achieves a state of bliss comparable in some fashion to that of Eden when Roboán, as Emperor of Triguida, has married Seringa. The author's plan may be roughly sketched in the following manner: first major *exemplum*, the earthly cleansing of man from the effects of original sin; second major *exemplum*, the demonstration of how man, by means of learning and wisdom, can maintain his status and further improve it; third major *exemplum*, the perfection of earthly society to the greatest possible extent achieved by following *redde quod debes* and the general tenor of the ideas expressed in the second *exemplum*.

The first and third *exempla* of the *Zifar* are typological in their effect in that the allegorical «meanings» implied by these sections are reflections or suggestions of important truths out of the drama of sacred history. Zifar's redemptive journey demonstrates that the force of Christ's life and message is constantly recurring in the lives of all men who follow Him. The attainment of the empire of Triguida by Roboán and his subsequent marriage to Seringa is suggestive of the forthcoming union of Christ and the Church in the Celestial Kingdom.

A. C. Charity has shown that certain parables and sayings of Jesus prove that «Jesus' present is being presented (and by himself) as realizing typologically the future of God» (147). In other words the New Testament actions of Christ foreshadow those events which will sum up human history and cast it into eternity in much the same way that certain Old Testament happenings presage Jesus' earthly doings. Christ's experience in this world is a type of the future planned by God for the human race and the «meaning» in both is the same. Typological signs alluding to man's forthcoming state of grace continue to be found in the Christian era, but types after Christ are subordinated both to His great example and its eventual fulfilment in and after the Second Coming. An event occurring in history after Jesus' return to heaven may be seen as recapitulating some happening in His life or it might foreshadow something from the end of time. Such an event taking place in the era between the great type of Christ's life and its equally glorious antitype (the Second Coming and the Celestial Kingdom) may reflect the configurations of either type, that is the actual point-by-point relation of what happened with Jesus, or antitype, that which is predicted to occur when He comes again. The «meaning» mirrored would be the same in either case because type and antitype of course have the same essential significance.

Zifar's adventures constitute a «subfulfilment» on this earth of that which is predicted by the ministry of Christ. The deeds of Roboán also are a «subfulfilment» [9] of the same ministry but the description of what happens to him is modeled upon the projected antitype to Christ (the Second Coming and the Celestial City) and not upon the real story of Jesus' life on earth. The *Castigos* section is figurally neutral in that it suggests no constant truths from sacred history but rather refers itself to the pragmatic «now». The author designed it as an allusion to certain absolute teachings of Christ—that man should heed Christian admonitions as a way to salvation. The first *exemplum* of the *Zifar* suggests what went before in Christian history; the third presages what is to come. The *Castigos* section is concerned with the present as it moves toward the predicted completion. It is typological only in the sense that it aids in establishing a terrestrial kingdom which is to be a prefigurement of the celestial one.

Each of the three *exempla* is illustrative of the theme *redde quod debes* in its own particular fashion. The first shows how man can return what he owes to God by modeling his life upon the virtuous example of Christ. The second argues that man can make recompense by striving to acquire learning and wisdom and by seeking to pass on what he gains to future generations. The third section again demonstrates that the man granted strength and virtue by the Almighty can repay the debt incurred by endeavoring to show himself as a dedicated *miles christi*.

Now it is possible to see how the literal and figural planes of the work function together to present the reader with a unified whole. The literal level, the story of virtuous men who live according to Christian ideas and ethics, provides the basis for the secondary stratum which is a sequence of suggestion and

[9] See Chapter Two, nn. 35 and 38.

implication construed to make the real lives of the heroes conform to certain archetypal patterns out of sacred history. The Middle Ages saw the great and worthy trajectory of Christ's deeds as influencing and molding human affairs until the end of time. Medieval man believed that the entire range of sacred history from the Creation until the Second Coming was centered upon Jesus' life. Because events in this life meant salvation for the world, the «meaning» implied in it would have the power to transform men's lives throughout the remainder of time. As A. C. Charity explains, history would conform itself «through grace to the pattern of Christ's history» (247). When Jesus said «If any man will come after me, let him deny himself, and take up his cross daily, and follow me» (Luke 9,23), he was stating that a conformity, metaphysical or true, would have to exist between the pattern of His earthly existence and that of every Christian. The Middle Ages preferred to see this conformity as a real parallelism, especially if the Christian involved were one particularly strong in his dedication to the precepts of the Master.

By carrying out the requisites of *redde quod debes* as knights and kings, Zifar and Roboán are in the fullest sense following the example of Christ. A parallel exists between their lives and that of the Saviour which the author of the *Zifar* wishes to show as one of true events and actions rather than attitude and belief. By means of his *emiendas*, he assimilates the stories of Zifar and Roboán to that of Jesus. Zifar's adventures conform typologically to Christ's life on earth; Roboán's feats suggest events, those of the Second Coming and beyond, which are yet to occur from the human point of view, but which are eternally and constantly present in the mind of God. As the reader follows the adventures of Zifar and his son, he simultaneously sees the pattern of what they do as repeating or predicting certain actions of Christ's. The effect is to demonstrate concretely how God's grace, spread out upon mankind through His Son, is ever capable of drawing men into the sacred economy of atonement and salvation.

It is also very probable that the three major *exempla* of the *Zifar*, which typologically refer to past, present, and future, suggest that most important of triune configurations, the Holy Trinity. It was common in the Middle Ages for writers to construct their works in such a manner so as to evoke trinitarian associations. [10] We have noted that the *Castigos* section is concerned with the imparting and preserving of knowledge and that the concept of «letradura» is portrayed in it as central to the well-being of human society. [11] It is the second person of the Trinity, the Son, who is identified with *sophia* or wisdom because the *logos* or divine Wisdom of God was that which was made flesh in the Incarnation. [12] Juan Manuel tells us that «saber complido es puesto a Dios Fijo», while «poder conplido es puesto a Dios Padre», and «vondat conplida, que es querer b[i]en conplido es puesto a Dios Spíritu Santo». [13] The second major *exemplum* of the *Zifar*, which so plainly deals with the imparting of wisdom, would logically seem to be connected with that concept of *sophia* which illustrates Christ's role as the incarnate *logos*. It follows that the other two *exempla* must reflect the Father and the Holy Ghost.

In the next chapter I note the resemblance between certain aspects of the millenarian thinking of the author of the *Zifar* and that of the Calabrian monk Joachim of Flora whose work influenced a number of writers in the later Middle Ages. One of Joachim's tenets was that there were three great world ages which corresponded to the figures of the Trinity. The last of these ages, that pertaining to the Holy Spirit, would see the flowering again briefly of the terrestrial paradise which would vanish before the last onrush of the antichrist just before the Second Coming. It is thus likely that the three *exempla* represent

[10]   As Juan Manuel indicates: «Mas estas tres cosas son [una] cosa, et todas son en un fecho que se faga. Et ninguna cosa non puede ser fecha conplida con que estas tres cosas non aya...» *(El libro enfenido,* 96). Berceo tells us that he constructed his *Vida de Santo Domingo de Silos* with three books or divisions in honor of the Trinity: «Como son tres personas e una Deidat, / que sean tres los libros, una certanidat, / los libros que signifiquen la Sancta Trinidat, / la materia ungada la simple Deidat» (534).

[11]   As in the *Divine Comedy:* «In the *Comedy,* no less than in his earlier works, Dante connects eloquence to wisdom and virtue, and therefore relates the state of language to the state of Christian society» (Colish, 328).

[12]   «One of the *arcana,* or rather obscure mysteries, of Christian mythology is the fact that the Son as Wisdom, Sophia, is *feminine* and that the Church also applies the passage from Proverbs (8.22, 31) to the Virgin Mary, since it is used as the Epistle of the Immaculate Conception. The great cathedral of Constantinople, Hagia Sophia, is of course dedicated to God the Son under this aspect» (Alan Watts, *Myth and Ritual in Christianity,* London and New York, 1954, 31). Juan Manuel at one point in *El libro enfenido* goes into a long elogium of the virtues of *saber* which he then connects to the Trinity: «Ca segund verdat, una de las tres cosas que son en la Trinidat, que es Dios Padre, et Fijo, [et] Spíritu Sancto, es el saber... saber complido es puesto a Dios Fijo» (95).

[13]   *Ibid.,* 95.

these three great world ages. [14]   In the eyes of the author of the *Zifar* the first, that figuring the Father, would be the period of redemption and recuperation of the loss suffered in Eden.   The second, analogous to the Son, would be the epoch when man would painfully learn the lessons apparent in God's word. The third would suggest the brief time of fruition promised in Isaiah and a part of Jewish and Christian eschatological lore which would prefigure the everlasting joys of the heavenly kingdom.   Here mankind, guided by the Holy Spirit, would realize his utmost potentially as a being created for salvation.

---

[14]   «This 'trinity' of ages would correspond to the divine Trinity and would satisfy a desire for order and rationality in history» (Morton Bloomfield, «Joachim of Flora», *Trad,* 13, 1957, 264).   Bloomfield goes on to point out that the idea of the «three ages» corresponding to the figures of the Trinity is absolutely logical if one considers the implications of the doctrine for Christians.   «The basic historical idea of Joachim, then, is very brilliant.   It carried... to a logical conclusion, in terms of a triune God, the basic idea of typology, which saw in the Old Testament a foreshadowing of the glory to come.   It combines the idea of cycle and pattern with the special concept of the unique and linear, which is characteristically historical» (269).

CHAPTER SEVEN

THE NEW EDEN

The third major *exemplum* in the *Zifar* treats the adventures of the youngest son of the family, Roboán, who leaves the peace and prosperity established in the kingdom of Mentón by his father, to follow his own quest to completion. The adventures of Zifar, an *imitatio Christi* which figures the personal redemption possible to each Christian as well as that of the human race, illustrate the possibilities open to humanity within the divine economy of the death and Resurrection of Christ. The *Castigos* section demonstrates how wisdom, accreted and retained through inspired language, must be passed on from father to son, increasing all the while, if man is to hold onto and go forward from the place he first reaches because of Christ's redemptive actions. The third section, continuing with this line of reasoning, shows how the gradual evolution, implied in the first two sections, would lead to a true earthly paradise, a «new age» which would foreshadow the bliss of the heavenly paradise. The whole panorama of Roboán's adventures is as emblematic of universal truths as were those of his father. The author of the *Zifar* telescopes into the scheme of «Los hechos de Roboán», by means of typological implication, the whole era of human progress from the time that man first walked into «newness of life» (implied in Zifar's adventures) until the moment of the Second Coming. Roboán stands as a figure for man living in a state of grace granted by Christ but still subject to the wiles of Satan who is ever hopeful of seducing the Christian into the paths of sin.

The history of messianic thought in the Middle Ages is a long and complicated one which ultimately relates back to Jewish sources and to the famous Sibylline prophecies of Byzantium.

9

Revolutionary eschatology had come into existence among the Jews after the First Captivity as a kind of defense mechanism by means of which they consoled and fortified themselves in times of great adversity. The Messiah was originally conceived as a wise and powerful leader of Davidic descent who would vanquish all foes and guide his people into a new era of peace and prosperity. As the political situation deteriorated for the Jews this longed-for ruler was slowly apotheosized into a superhuman individual who would win his victories by means of direct divine intervention.[1] The Sibylline prophecies took the essence of this Jewish Messiah and applied it to the person of the Roman Emperor. Later the Christian Middle Ages which inherited the tradition of the Sibyllines never tired of hoping that a great ruler, combining the attributes of David with those of the Caesars, would come forth to establish a kingdom of peace and justice upon this earth as a prelude to the Second Coming of Christ. Toward the end of the medieval epoch this expectation was so powerful that Christians tried to see the Last Emperor in any king who was crowned and chroniclers hopefully alluded to every new monarch as *rex justus* or David.[2]

One of the better known, and most systematically organized of the exponents of chiliastic thinking in the later Middle Ages, was the Calabrian monk Joachim of Flora who envisaged a final age of gold which would follow the defeat of Antichrist by a great ruler. Joachim believed that he had discovered seven parallel ages of development, one in the Old Testament, the other in the New, which were alluded to in the Seven Seals of the Apocalypse. Superimposed upon these sevens were three great world ages which corresponded to the figures of the Trinity. There had been a period free from disruptive strife in the seventh epoch of the Old Testament which was a premonition, a typological foretaste, of that great glory to ensue in the seventh era of New Testament time when the Holy Spirit would truly reign.[3] A point of critical importance in Joachim's thought is that he did not believe that this period of peace and prosperity would lead directly and immediately into the Parousia. To have

[1] See Norman Cohn, *The Pursuit of the Millenium* (London, 1962), 4.
[2] *Ibid.,* 20.
[3] See M. Reeves and B. Hirsch-Reich, «The Seven Seals of Joachim of Fiore», *RTAM,* 21 (1954), 217.

asserted this would have been to almost equate this period of accomplishment within time to that blessedness which was to reign outside of time in the celestial city. What Joachim did was to place the battle with the most terrible Antichrist, or Antichrists, [4] before the moment of earthly renovation. But because of man's sin, never completely removed from this world, even this golden age would terminate with strife and disruption and the appearance of one final minion of Satan whose defeat would signal the Second Coming. [5] By having this period of peace and justice degenerate into disharmony, Joachim could avoid what surely would have been labelled as heretical. At the same time he was able to suggest what he saw to be definitely predicted in Scripture, a time of great earthly amelioration which would return man nearly to the conditions of the lost Eden.

Because Joachim had not prejudiced Biblical tradition by predicting an absolute and complete betterment of mankind before Christ's Second Advent, orthodox writers and thinkers throughout the later Middle Ages were to use his schemes as models for their own messianic systems. In Spain both Ramon Lull and Arnald of Villanova exemplify various aspects of the chiliastic tradition. Lull believed that it was possible to revive the vague memory of the Roman Empire and use it as a model upon which to construct a new imperium unifying all mankind in a «cruzada espiritual» toward the realization of utopia upon the earth. [6] Arnald, who was a follower of Joachim of Flora, lacked any political vision [7] and asserted that «la reforma social florecerá, más que por el esfuerzo de las capas populares, por la tarea dirigente e inspirada del representante de Cristo en la tierra». [8]

Unfortunately it seems impossible, at least at the present time, to trace and relate the various aspects of messianic thinking in medieval Europe. Bloomfield's suggestion that all such ideas may reflect not an organized system of thought but more a particular *Zeitgeist*, [9] prevalent for a thousand years, may provide

---

[4] Joannes de Rupescissa (Jean de Roquetaillade) and many other medieval thinkers viewed the Antichrist as multiple. See M. Reeves, «Joachimist Influences on the Idea of a Last World Emperor», *Trad*, 17 (1961), 328-329.

[5] *Ibid.*, 324.

[6] Joaquín and Tomás Carreras y Artau, *Historia de la filosofía española* (Madrid, 1939-1943), 625.

[7] *Ibid.*, 229.

[8] *Ibid.*, 228.

[9] Morton Bloomfield, «Joachim of Flora», mentions the multitude of medieval

the most suitable explanation for the confusing currents and crosscurrents which characterize the whole of medieval thought concerning social reform. Understanding the situation in Spain is as perplexing and difficult as comprehending what went on elsewhere. The author of the *Zifar*, writing in the era of Juan Manuel just after the great cultural flowering of the time of Alfonso X, would undoubtedly have known Lull, Villanova, and perhaps Joachim of Flora as well. But due to an incomplete understanding of the social message of Lull and Villanova, not to speak of Joachim, it is impossible to exactly relate those elements of messianic thinking present in the *Zifar* to the tradition preceding it.

The author of the work appears to use, for example, concepts similar both to Lull's idea of the imperium, which of course must itself relate in some way to the Sibylline prophecies, and to Villanova's conception of Christ's personal representative as the reformer of mankind. Zifar and Roboán are individual agents of Divinity in improving their lots and thereby that of their subjects. In the third *exemplum* Roboán realizes the *paradisus regnum* in the figure of the Empire of Triguida, the very name of which suggests that the earthly equivalent of the forthcoming celestial kingdom has been achieved (442). It is possible that he borrowed these ideas from Lull and Villanova, but it is more likely that he found suggestions of them in the atmosphere of millenial hope and expectation which characterized the High Middle Ages.

Joachim's theory of history however is more directly helpful in explaining one of the perplexing aspects of the organization of the *Zifar*. If the work is based upon sermon structure, and if its three natural divisions constitute the major *exempla* expected in a university homily, the reader anticipates that these *exempla* will provide some sort of development of the sermonic theme which in the *Zifar* is the axiom *redde quod debes*. For a king the obvious fulfilment of this precept is the founding of a kingdom in which Christian principles guide both ruler and subjects. In line with the explanation given of the meaning of the *exempla*,

thinkers and writers who had ideas similar to those of Joachim and he queries whether it is possible to think that Joachim had read these writers or whether he merely shared in a *Zeitgeist* prevalent in the era (280). Bloomfield does point out Joachim's unique contribution to the tradition—the idea of a new age of the Holy Ghost as a final earthly fulfilment (280).

that the first illustrates man's symbolic liberation from the effects of original sin and the Old Law, that the second shows man's slow progress through the accretion and passing-on of knowledge, and that the third presents the highest plane of existence possible to humanity on this earth, the author of the *Zifar* might have been expected to portray this progression in linear fashion. Instead he seems to have broken the sequence by creating a *paradisus regnum* at the end of the first *exemplum*, the kingdom of Mentón. This asymmetrical development becomes logical if the reader relates the author of the *Zifar*'s pattern to that one perceived in history by Joachim of Flora. At the very end of the Old Testament, the era of the Old Law, Joachim had seen a brief *renovatio* which was a type of the final and greatest period of earthly regeneration. Doubtless Joachim's idea was that both appearances of Christ, the first and the second, had to be preceded by epochs of amelioration.

The author of the *Zifar* has incorporated some such vista into his work. The kingdom of Mentón might be taken as corresponding to that renewal which Joachim posited for the end of the Old Law which is symbolized in the *Zifar* by the knight's journey from Tarta to Mentón. The second *renovatio*, the Empire of Triguida, by its very name a new Eden, is the one leading to and preparing the way for the Second Advent of Christ and the establishment of His kingdom.

The critic, of course, might argue that the author of the *Zifar* has created an absurdity with his two renewals in historical time after Christ's first Coming. His *renovatio* in Triguida can be explained, but if Christ has already come and gone once, then there can be no reason for a period of peace and harmony in Mentón as a preparation for that first Advent. The answer is that medieval man thought in patterns. Just as the first *exemplum* is based upon the model of Christ's earthly life, so the entire work is a telescoping of all human history from the Fall to the moment preceding the Second Coming. [10] In the *Zifar* the

---

[10] An excellent example of how medieval man searched for and found divinely inspired time patterns in every aspect of his life may be seen in Durandus who allegorically interprets the four seasons as a model upon which all other periods of time are based. While explicating the significance of the liturgical year, Durandus comments upon the curious fact that Advent, based upon the type of spring, precedes Septuagesima-Lent which represents the winter of sin. Immediately following the Resurrection, the Fifty Days figures the summer of human affairs which looks forward to the celestial kingdom. Advent has to come first he says, because Christ has

author shows how the trajectory of meaning impressed upon time by God's Will is ever and constantly replaying itself in the lives of individual Christians. The final demonstration of what this meaning is and how it affects the lives of men comes in the third *exemplum* where the ultimate illustration of the sermonic theme *redde quod debes* simultaneously occurs.

The most important clue which aids us in comprehending the meaning implied in the third section comes from the word Roboán itself. It is obvious that the author has borrowed the name from the son of Solomon who was king after his father and who threatened to «chasten the people of Israel with Scorpions», [11] since this famous intimidation is mentioned in the work (307). Because Rehoboam took the advice of young counselors, instead of that of older and wiser ones, he departed from the way of the Lord with the result that the Kingdom of David was divided into the ten tribes of Israel and the two tribes of Judah and Benjamin. The Middle Ages never grew tired of moralizing on his precipitate actions, pointing out that Rehoboam's deeds were archetypal for any young king who was not careful to heed the advice of seasoned and honest sages. [12] Because of his grandfather David's loyalty, God did not see fit to banish his house from the throne of Israel completely, but promised, as Jonas of Orleans says, to leave some descendant in Jerusalem forever. It is of course from this line that Christ comes to live a short time upon this earth and then to become a heavenly king.

With the name Roboán, the author of the *Zifar* is able to demonstrate two important points: first, he can portray the son of Zifar as a kind of positive antitype to the son of Solomon. [13] Whereas Rehoboam did not heed the advice of wise counselors,

died, thereby establishing the primacy of faith, hope, and charity. The winter period is necessary because sin remains in the world. But it is a knowledge of sin tempered by the assurance provided by Advent-spring that a summer must be very near (III, 145). Thus the Church precipitously jumps from winter (Holy Week) into summer (the Fifty Days) with the Easter Resurrection.

[11] I Kings 12.11.

[12] «Propter piaculum enim Salomonis domus Israel Dominus de manibus filiorum ejus dispersit, et propter meritum David regis lucernam de semine ejus semper in Hierusalem reliquit» (Jonas of Orleans, *PL*, 106, 289). For basically the same idea in Spain see Juan Manuel, *El libro enfenido*, 115.

[13] Thus Roboán reverses his prefiguration, the first Rehoboam in the book of Kings. This is of course the classic interpretation of Christ's deeds as the reversal within history of the behaviour of Adam. See Burlin, *The Old English Advent*, 8.

the new Roboán would do so. More important, Solomon's
son saw his kingdom divided against him because, filled with
pride and anger, he had threatened his people with an even
heavier yoke than that imposed by his father. Zifar's son will
also commit a grievous error owing to cupidity and will lose the
kingdom of the Islas Dotadas granted to him by God's intermediary Fortune. [14] But the effect is not this time permanent
because in the intervening historical time Christ has died for
man's sins. Thus when Roboán repents, he is free to rise to
become the Emperor of Triguida. The second point is that just
as Christ, a descendant of David as foretold in prophecy, [15]
will secure man's eternal salvation so Roboán, by his name also
an offshoot of the royal house of Israel, will consolidate the
earthly commonwealth.

Roboán's name in Hebrew, as most medieval exegetes were
aware, meant *latitudo* or *impetus populi*. Most commentators
were of course struck by the divergence between the promise
implied in his name and the reality of his deeds. A few, such
as Rabanus Maurus in *Commentariorum in Matthaeum*, interpreted
the force of the meaning of *latitudo* or *impetus populi* in a purely
allegorical manner unrelated to the circumstances of Roboán's
life. [16] Far more common was the explanation that the meaning
latitudo populi should be taken as an example of the rhetorical
figure *antiphrasis*—the giving of a name to something which
indicates the opposite of its qualities. [17]

The author of the *Zifar* seems to have decided to return to the
true sense of the appelation as it was without recourse to *antiphrasis* or exaggerated allegorical interpretation. It was doubtless
the intent of Solomon that his son should possess the qualities
implied in the word Roboán and it was one of those awful ac-
cidents of human destiny, brought on by sin, that the son did
not fulfil the expectation of the father. On an earthly plane the
advent of Rehoboam meant the end of the peace and prosperity
of the Kingdom of David which had been endangered but not
ruined by Solomon, whose name, also somewhat antiphrastically,

[14]   See Burke, *HR*, XXXVIII (1970), 56-68.
[15]   See Porubcan, 511-512 and 562-563.
[16]   Roboán, *impetus populi mei* interpretatur, et significat velocem conventum
populorum ad fidem Christi post incarnationem ejus» (*PL*, 107, 740).
[17]   See Rabanus Maurus, *PL*, 110, 462-463 and Christianus Druthmarus, *PL*, 106,
1270-1271.

means the peaceful one. The author of the *Zifar* saw an opportunity to reestablish the qualities of the Davidic kingdom once more upon the earth by having a new member of this royal line arise who would in his kingdom and in his time bring the heritage bequeathed to him by his father to fruition rather than despair. Zifar, another David, the name of whose kingdom must derive from Psalm 132v, establishes a reign of peace and harmony. [18] The implication is that both his sons Garfín and Roboán will continue the father's work, the older son in Mentón and Roboán in Triguida. This time the earthly kingdom will not be lost to the descendants of David but will prosper.

Roboán's first chivalrous adventure during his quest occurs in the land of Pandulfa where Seringa rules. She has inherited the kingdom from her father, but finds that she is unable to protect it from her avaricious neighbors, the kings of Brez and Grimalet. I have attempted to show elsewhere that Pandulfa is an etymological equivalent to the name Galapia in the first *exemplum* where Zifar saves a widowed ruler. [19] Galapia meant «the action of seizing something by force» in Arabic. [20] The word «pantoufla», evidently the etymon from which the author of the *Zifar* took his name for Seringa's beleaguered land, means «to grab» or «to seize» in Provençal. [21] The names of both lands suggest the unchivalrous actions of the attackers in attempting to take something by force from helpless women. The word Seringa is derived from Arabic *sharika* «wife» or «woman partner». Much later when Roboán as Emperor of Triguida returns to Pandulfa to marry her the idea implied in her name is fulfilled.

Once the young knight has succeeded in delivering Pandulfa from the evil kings, Seringa and her uncle, Ruben, try to persuade him to remain with them as her husband and protector. Roboán is insistent, however, that he must complete his mission before he can marry. Seringa begs him to return for her after finishing his quest and promises to wait for him for three years (429).

Having helped the Count of Turbia to settle his quarrel with his subjects, the young knight travels on and finally reaches the land of Triguida which, the author tells us, takes its name from

---

[18] See Chapter Four, where I discuss Mentón.
[19] See *RR*, 69 (1968), 170.
[20] *Ibid.*, 165-166.
[21] *Ibid.*, 170.

the River Triguis «uno de los quatro rios que salen del parayso terreñal» (442). Roboán, by setting out upon and persevering in his quest has returned to, or near to, the very place whence Adam and Eve fled after being expelled from Eden. Because of his fulfilment of this «demanda» and due to «sus buenas costunbres e porquel quiso Dios por la su bondat guiar» (444), he will one day become ruler over the entire Empire of Triguida. Roboán quickly becomes the favorite of the Emperor of the land who not only knights him again according to the local custom but also decides to make the deserving young man his heir.

The author of the *Zifar* is not content to have Roboán become an emperor without illustrating how the road of life can be especially full of peril for a prince. Man was freed from the bondage of original sin by the death and Resurrection of Christ, but he was not secured from the influences of Satan. In fact, as I have pointed out, [22] medieval tradition held that the Christian was most in danger at that very moment when he had turned toward the newness of life. Thus Roboán, the most fortunate of young men, is most vulnerable to sin at just the time when he seems ready to realize the objectives for which he had set out.

Seven evil counts who are jealous of his influence with the Emperor, trick him into asking a forbidden question—why the Emperor never laughs. As a result the Emperor, to punish him and also to test him, places him in an enchanted boat which whisks him away across the sea to the Islas Dotadas which the author of the *Zifar* has conceived as the abode of Fortune. There he marries the lovely Nobleza, ruler of the Islands and probably the very daughter of Chance herself. He is happy and content with his new wife for almost a year until he again falls victim to temptation, this time much more serious than the mild *curiositas* which resulted in his asking the Emperor the forbidden question. The devil, disguised as a beautiful girl, tricks the young knight into requesting Nobleza to give him a powerful horse, a symbol of *luxuria* and *cupiditas*. Because of his unbounded greed in desiring something which Nobleza had warned was too strong for him, he is carried by the horse to the edge of the sea, thrown into a boat, and ferried back again to Triguida where the Emperor awaits him on the shore.

[22] See Chapter Four, nn. 17-18.

Roboán lost the enchanted kingdom of the Islas Dotadas because he allowed inordinate desires to better him. «E este, commoquier que era mucho entendido en todas cosas, e mucho aperçebido e de grant coraçon, non sopo guardarse de los engaños e de las maestrias del diablo, que se trabaja sienpre de engañar los omes para los fazer perder las almas e la onrra deste mundo» (480). But the result of the experience was good in that it demonstrated most strongly to Roboán how he, as a future king, could fall victim to the same kind of temptations and lose much more. The Emperor of Triguida, himself a victim of similar adventures in the Islas Dotadas, urges Roboán to perceive the example apparent in his misfortune and benefit by it. «'Bien aya mal', dixo el enperador, 'que trae tan grant virtud consigo que de los tristes faze alegres e da entendimiento a ome para se saber guardar mejor en las cosas quel acaesçieren; ca este diablo maldito nos fizo sabidores para nos guardar de yerro o de non creer por todas cosas que nos acometan con falagueras palabras e engañosas...'» (483-484).

Roboán is a nearly perfect knight who begins his quest in the comfort of his father's kingdom of Mentón. There was nothing in his life or environment to remind him of those still valid consequences of man's iniquities which had been so apparent to his father while caught in the shadows of Tarta. The author of the *Zifar* has conceived the Islas Dotadas episode as a way of proving to the young knight that he, as well as all other men, must be constantly on guard or else run the risk of falling prey to Satan. [23] The sin that engineers his downfall is the one, along with pride, which was considered in the Middle Ages to be the root of all evil particularly in things having to do with government. «E el mesquino non sopo guardar el bien e la onrra en que estava, por codiçia de cosas muy escusadas sy el quesiera» (480). [24]

[23] Bernard Levy points out the same thing in regard to Sir Gawain in *Sir Gawain and the Green Knight*: «For Gawain proves to be the nearly perfect Christian knight—as nearly as mere man can be, as every good Christian must strive to be—but he must be reminded of the tendency to sin incurred by the inheritance of original sin» («Gawain's Spiritual Journey», 104).

[24] Robertson in *Preface to Chaucer* points out that Concupiscence, together with a concomitant defect in reason, is the predominant form which original sin takes in the Middle Ages (27). The idea that cupidity is the root of all evil in the state is commonplace in the medieval world, but an excellent example of the viewpoint may be found in Hincmar of Rheims, *PL,* 125, 833-856 and 983-1018. The scribe who incorporated much of the *Regimiento de príncipes* of Egidio Romano

Not long after Roboán does indeed become Emperor of Triguida, the author gives him the opportunity to fight against and defeat personifications of a group of minor sins which are closely allied to his major transgression. Scarcely has he ascended the throne when he is faced with rebellion and sedition fomented by the same seven counts who had tricked him into asking the former Emperor why he never laughed (485). These seven evil counts plant fear in the hearts of his vassals, especially the Kings of Safira and Garba, and cause them to join in the uprising against the young Emperor. The name Garba derives from Arabic *karb* «worry», «care», or «grief» and is indicative of the lack of courage in the weak vassal. The leader of the counts and the one who has been most influential in planting suspicion and thereby causing the revolt is Count Farán. «... e porque non nos sopiemos guardar del mal consejo, e señaladamente del conde Faran... ca el y los otros condes... nos metieron en muy grant miedo e grant sospecha de vos» (501). The name Farán comes from the Arabic verb *fara*—to invent lyingly, fabricate, trump up something against. Count Farán, the true instigator of the rebellion, is a personification of *mendacium*, a sin viewed by medievals as particularly insidious for those playing instrumental roles in government in that it was generally a primary step toward treason. The author of the *Zifar* himself twice presents *mentira* as the first of a series of vices which lead up to «daño de todas las cosas del mundo» (511). [25]

into a manuscript of the *Castigos e documentos* was aware that the following lines provide warning against cupidity: «...así como el amor de Dios é del bien comun trae al home á virtudes, así el amor desordenado de sí mesmo trae al home á todos los males é á todos los pecados. Et así los reys se deben guardar de non amar el bien propio mas que el bien divinal é el bien comun: ca por esto fueron denostados é menospreciados muchos reys» (ed. Pascual de Gayangos, 188). According to Agapito Rey this section of the manuscript which Gayangos edited is an interpolation of the *Regimiento de príncipes;* see Rey's edition of the *Castigos e documentos,* 11.

[25] Morton Bloomfield, *The Seven Deadly Sins* (East Lansing, 1952), points out that two medieval commentators on the Seven Deadly Sins add an eighth sin, lying, which is probably based on the biblical authority of James 3.2 ff (87, 124). The author of the *Zifar,* following the *Poridat de las poridades,* twice lists *mentira* as the first of a series of vices which leads up to «crueldat... destruymiento de toda natura de ome...» (305, 311). The list is *mentira* which breeds *discordia* which breeds *despagamiento* and so on through *injuria, departimiento de amor, aborrençia, guerra, enemistad, batalla* finally to *crueldat*. The list on 311 is slightly altered and abbreviated but is basically the same. It is possible that a chain of vices starting from *mendacium* represented a kind of popular «deadly sins of society» which paralleled the well-known seven which are more individually oriented. The popular reasoning in regard to lying as a danger to the commonwealth can be seen

The sin of lying was seen throughout the Middle Ages as issuing forth from the closely allied capital sins of *cupiditas*, *avaritia* and *luxuria*. [26] Hugh of St. Victor, for example, in a fascinating configuration, which resembles the author of the *Zifar*'s concept of *cupiditas* as the origin of *mendacium*, makes avarice the overlord of seven counts, three of whose names suggest the sin of *mendacium*.

> Avaritia est gloriae divitarum seu quarum libet aliarum rerum insatiabilis et inhonesta cupiditas. Ejus comites sunt philargyria perjurium, violentia, usura, fraus, rapina et fallacia... Perjurium est fraudulentia commodi consequendi aut damni devitandi gratia, veritatis agnitae abnegatio pejeranda facta... Fraus est per quam familiari rei, inopiae causa, clandestina subreptione consulitur... Fallacia est per quam motibus deceptionis veritas rei palliatur vel odium alterius vel proprium commodum intenditur. [27]

Roboán fell victim to the overwhelming power of cupidity and thereby lost the Islas Dotadas. Now he must in some way come to terms with himself and reestablish a firm and lasting control over his inordinate desires. The author presents the struggle which he must fight against the lingering results of *cupiditas* as a real battle in the style which had originated with the *Psychomachia*. [28] The seven counts represent sins closely connected in medieval thinking with treason and harm to the commonwealth. Roboán defeats these personified sins with the aid of a wonderful banner which had been given to him by Nobleza shortly before he was torn from her by the horse. It is clear from the author's description of the scene where he finds it that it symbolizes the power and efficacy of the seven virtues.

> ... e finco los ynojos e saco el pendon con grant devoçion, llorando de los ojos, ca tenia que pues aquella bos del çielo desçendia e le

in a translation of the Penitential of Bartholomew Iscanus (1161-1184): «He who knowingly commits perjury also either disbelieves or neglects the sanctity of the whole Christian profession, since an oath constitutes the end of every controversy in ecclesiastical affairs, and in secular matters many controversies are terminated by an oath» (quoted in John T. McNeill and Helena Gamer, *Medieval Handbooks of Penance*, New York, 1938, 349).

[26] Vincent of Beauvais has a work listed under *luxuria* called *De vitiis linguae* the first of which is *mendacium* (*The Seven Deadly Sins*, 126). The Penitential of Silos links cupidity immediately to perjury. «But he who through cupidity willfully perjures himself shall serve God in a monastery until death, his goods being given to the poor» (McNeill and Gamer, 287).

[27] *PL*, 176, 1001.

[28] See Post, 105-107.

fizo emiente del pendon, que grant virtud avia en el. E asy era;
ca aquellas syete donzellas quel pendon fizieron, bien avia cada una
setenta años, ca en tienpo de su avuela de la enperatris, nasçieron
todas de un vientre, e ella las crio. E las donzellas fueron sienpre de
tan buena vida que non quisieron casar, mas prometieron castidat, e
mantovieronla muy bien e muy santamente, de guisa que Dios fazia
por ellas en aquel inperio muchos miraglos, e nunca labravan cosa
por sus manos en que Dios non puso señaladamente su virtud (499).

By taking and using the banner made by these seven pure maidens,
who must represent the seven virtues, Roboán becomes their
vassal. [29] The author of the *Zifar* is saying that the young
knight will overcome the rebellious lords, who are symbols
of sins issuing from his cupidity, by means of a banner emblematic
of the seven virtues. [30]

Once Roboán has quieted the commonwealth by winning
symbolic victory over the rebellious counts, it is logical that he
begin to think of marrying so that an heir can be provided for
the kingdom. He recalls the promise which he had made to
Seringa before leaving Pandulfa and dispatches el Cavallero Amigo
to ask her to come to Triguida so that they may be married.

Prior to this point in the third *exemplum* the author of the
Zifar has made no mention of the liturgical date, the observance
of which was of capital importance in the first major *exemplum*.
From now on he begins to carefully set each happening in his
sequence of events according to the Church calendar. Seringa
orders all her vassals to come to her palace during the week
after the Octave of Easter so that she can inform them of her

[29] For example when Louis VI carried the banner of St. Denis into battle he
became the vassal of the abbot who was the representative of the saint (Von
Simson, 71).

[30] Edwin B. Place sees this same sort of struggle between a knight representing
the virtues and the Seven Deadly Sins in the *Amadís* (III, 930). Robert Kaske,
«Dante's 'DXV' and 'Veltro'», discusses the difficulty which Dante faced in elim-
inating the wolf of concupiscence which appears early in the *Inferno* and comes
to the conclusion that Dante reached the most satisfactory solution possible which
was «...a regeneration ending in the one period since the Fall that might possibly
be conceived of as freed from the wolf of *concupiscentia,* with the Church on earth
already purified for her ascent to the divine *Sponsus*» (248). The author of the
Zifar eliminates his «wolf of *concupiscentia*», which Roboán encountered not in
lupine form but in the horse in the Islas Dotadas, once the young knight has won
victory over the rebellious vassals. Now the way is clear for the marriage to
Seringa and the subsequent establishment of the «tierra de bendiçion» in Triguida
as the prototype of the heavenly kingdom. Both Dante and the author of the
Zifar found the solutions to the problem of *concupiscentia* and *cupiditas* in the world
by presenting them as symbolic animals and then having their heroes react against
these symbols.

desire to marry Roboán. Immediately afterwards she leaves for Triguida where she arrives on Pentecost. Later she and Roboán are married on the feast of St. John the Baptist in a city called Lédica.

Since the liturgical date was of such great importance in pointing to deeper significance in the first *exemplum*, it is reasonable that the calendar might also signal broader meaning in «Los hechos de Roboán». As I noted previously, the name Seringa must derive from Arabic *sharika* which meant «wife» or «female partner». The Freytag Latin-Arabic Dictionary lists the *Kamous*, an influential 10th century lexicon, as giving the word *shurka* or *shirka*, a close etymological complement to *sharika*, with the meaning *societas* or *communio*. If the three Arabic radicals *sh*, *r*, and *k* possess in some circumstances the force of «society» or «communion»,[31] it is possible that the author of the *Zifar* may have been using the name Seringa to signal a meaning of greater consequence than merely female partner or wife. I would suggest that the marriage of Roboán and Seringa represents in earthly terms the necessary joining of Church and State into one resolute *corpus mysticum* which will serve as a prefiguration of those sacred nuptials predestined for the end of time when Christ will come to earth seeking His bride the Church. Just as this union denotes the beginning of the celestial paradise which will endure for eternity, so the wedding of Roboán and Seringa would indicate the achievement of a second earthly Eden which would lead up to and foreshadow its heavenly counterpart. The author of the *Zifar* constructs this meaning within the text via an elaborate series of figural allusions, as complex as those used in the first *exemplum*, which underscore his illustration of the workings of divine redemption.

Just as Lent, the period preceding Easter, is the time which liturgically commemorates man's bondage to sin, so the «Fifty Days» which stretch from Easter Sunday to Pentecost symbolizes humanity's freedom from Satan and also the fruits of that freedom, the Resurrection and Christ's heavenly kingdom.[32] Pentecost,

[31] See G. W. Freytag, *Lexicon Arabico-Latinum*, II (Halle, 1830), 415.
[32] Prosper Guéranger, *L'Année liturgique* (Paris, 1911) in his description of the post-Paschal season says that it was at that time that Adam was formed and placed in the Garden of Eden and likewise that the general Resurrection would occur in the same period (8, 71-72). Gregory Dix, *The Shape of the Liturgy,* says that the Fifty Days manifest the «world to come» (340). Figure XIX of Joachim

the descent of the Holy Ghost upon the Apostles, was «the feast of the end of time, of the Church Triumphant». [33] Within the spectrum of human history the Church looked upon the Fifty Days and the great feast which ended it as the period when the Holy Spirit, once again visited upon mankind, would begin to effect the kingdom of God upon the earth. [34]

The union of the earthly and the divine symbolized by a nuptial ceremony is a metaphor which has been widely used throughout history to indicate that a state of harmony has been achieved in human affairs. [35] During the Middle Ages any marriage was understood as a figure for Christ's mystical oneness with the Church, and also could be used to imply the unity of the spiritual and temporal realms upon this earth even if in reality Church and State tended to go their separate ways. [36] To make this symbolic union more comprehensible in human terms princes sometimes «married» the Church of their dominion during the

---

of Flora's *Liber Figurarum* gives «Dies Pentecostes» parallel to «Dies unus eternus qui nullo temporum clauditur fine» (*Il Libro delle Figure,* ed. Leone Tondelli, Marjorie Reeves and Beatrice Hirsch-Reich, II, Torino, 1953). The liturgy during the Fifty Days is full of expectation for the forthcoming celestial kingdom. Cf. the 2nd antiphon of Matins for the IV Sunday after Easter in the Gothic Breviary: «Elegit nos hereditatem sibi rex omnis terrae Deus. *Response.* Regnavit Dominus omnis terrae: et inhabitabitur universa terra. P. Ut paradisus circumcinges omnem terram» (*PL,* 86). The explicator of the liturgy, Amalarius, tells us what the Fifty Days meant to the medieval: «Illi dies quinquaginta qui secuntur a sabbato paschali usque ad octavas pentecostes, alteram vitam informant, quam nondum percepimus, ibi non erit responsorius, quis nemo ibi praedicabitur, sed erunt omnes docibilies Dei; neque aliquus visitabitur, quis nemo ibi vidua, nemo pupillus, neque infirmus; elemosina non erit necessaria, quia nemo ibi indigens; sed tantum alleluia ibi celebrabitur, id est laetitia animarum de percepta inmortalitate et receptione corporum, et gratiarum actio Deo in sempiternum. Eandem laetitiam numerus quinquagenarius significat, qui apud Ebreos iubelius appellabitur, id est iubelatione plenus» (*Liber officialis* in *Opera liturgica omnia,* ed. Ioannus Michaelus Hanssens, II, Vatican City, 1948, 171-172).

[33] Morton Bloomfield, «Piers Plowman as a Fourteenth-Century Apocalypse», in *Interpretations of Piers Plowman,* ed. by Edward Vasta (Notre Dame, Ind. and London, 1968), 344.

[34] See Guéranger III, 356. Jean Daniélou points out that the Sacraments which Christ had instituted during His earthly life did not become effective until Pentecost when the Holy Spirit made their force active in the lives of Christians (*Jean Baptiste,* Paris, 1964, 129).

[35] See Ananda K. Coomaraswamy, *Spiritual Authority and Temporal Power* (New Haven, 1942), 84 for an explanation of how marriage has been used ritually to indicate the beginning of a new order, both terrestrial and divine.

[36] «Onde el matrimonio es señal é significa muy santa cosa, ca significa el ayuntamiento de la divinidat con la humanidat en Jesucristo, que es muy santa cosa, é aun significa el ayuntamiento de Jesucristo con la Iglesia» (*Castigos e documentos,* ed. Pascual de Gayangos, 209). This quote is also from the portion of the *Regimiento de príncipes* (see note 24, above).

coronation ceremony. [37] The state of uniformity and repose
suggested by these all-encompassing nuptials would foreshadow
the forthcoming bliss to be attained after the final non-mystically
understood union of the Church Triumphant with Christ following the Parousia.

Despite the fact that Church and State indulged in a long and
enduring struggle for supremacy down to the 14th century, there
was never any question but that both comprised a whole. [38]
It was the usual pettiness of human nature which refused to
develop an effective formula by which the two could exist together as one. Neither side in the long quarrel ever seriously
questioned that Christ had meant that all facets of society,
religious and secular, formed together the *Corpus Christi*. The
theory of coordinate powers or «the two swords» was only a
compromise at best by which neither Church nor State intruded
too much upon the other for fear of swift retaliation. I have previously pointed out that the author of the *Zifar* pays perfunctory
lip-service to the «two swords» idea (312-313) but in reality belies
the theory when he says that king, people, and clergy must
adhere to one law which in the end derives from the secular
ruler. «... e quando la opinion de los omes es una, ayunta los
coraçones de los omes en amor e tuelle muchos daños; e porende
el rey e el saçerdote e el pueblo deven convenir a una ley en lo
que ovieron a fazer e de creer...» (313). The king should «demandar consejo al saçerdote» in regard to what he should do,
but nowhere does the author of the *Zifar* hint that the secular
ruler must *abide* by these *consejos*. How different the political
philosophy of kingship in Spain was in the days following Alfonso X from that of Frederick II in Sicily who envisaged a purely
secular state free from spiritual authority yet vitalised by spiritual
forces [39] is a matter which deserves serious attention from
students of medieval political science. It is likely that Alfonso,
in order to set up an effective legal and administrative system in
readiness for his ascent to the Imperial throne, assimilated the

[37] See Emile Mâle, *L'Art religieuse du XIIᵉ siècle* (Paris, 1922), 198.
[38] Although the Roman Church was never able to achieve a theocracy such as
that which ruled in the Muslim world (cf. Gustave von Grunebaum, *Medieval Islam,*
Chicago, 1946, 154), the idea that Church and State were one remained a basic principle of medieval thought. See Chroust, «The Corporate Idea», and Petry, *Christian
Eschatology,* 266, 273, 275, and 276.
[39] Kantorowicz, *Frederick II,* 229.

greater part of Frederick's political thinking for his own use. [40]
Whatever the case may be the relationship suggested in the *Zifar*
between *regnum* and *sacerdotium* bears great resemblance to that
evolved by Frederick II.

Common also in medieval thought was the figure of the
Prince's nuptial attachment to the kingdom which he was going
to rule. Ernst Kantorowicz has studied and traced the history
of the phrase «le roy espousa solemnellement le royaume» which
was introduced into the French Coronation Order at the acces-
sion of Henry II in 1547 and has found that, far from being
merely an attractive metaphor, the formula was in agreement
with a long and distinguished tradition. [41] Kantorowicz traces
this custom back to the South Italian jurist Lucas de Penna
(born ca. 1320) who evidently used the old metaphor of the
marriage of the bishop to his see (based on Ephesians 5.25) in
a new context to apply to the relationship between the prince
and his realm. Although Lucas was writing some years after
the date of the *Zifar*, it seems likely that the idea which is first
found concretely stated in his work might have existed earlier.
As an offshoot of Aristotle's doctrine of human society, Kantorowicz concludes that the political entity (prince and state) had
copied the philosophy and nomenclature previously reserved
for Christ and his *corpus ecclesiae mysticum*. «Thus, the venerable
image of *sponsus* and *sponsa*, Christ and His Church, was transferred
from the spiritual to the secular and adapted to the jurist's need
for defining the relations between Prince and State.» [42]

The author of the *Zifar* in the *Castigos* section follows the
Flores de filosofia in equating the ruler and his kingdom with two
persons united in one. «Ca el rey e su regno son dos personas,
e asy commo una cosa ayuntada dos en uno» (318). It seems
likely that the author has illustrated this idea of the prince and
his realm being «una cosa ayuntada dos en uno» by presenting
it in terms of the marriage of Roboán (the king) to Seringa (the

---

[40] «What the world, however, seized upon, and what each of the European
states sooner or later, directly or indirectly, adopted was the technique of statecraft
which Frederick had deduced from his metaphysics... The maxims of state in time
asserted themselves everywhere; first, of course, in the neighbouring Romance
kingdoms, in France and Aragon as well as in divided Italy, perhaps in Castille too,
even before the end of the century» (*Ibid.*, 271).

[41] Ernst Kantorowicz, «Mysteries of State: An Absolutist Concept and its Late
Medieval Origins», *HTR*, 48 (1955), 65-91, at p. 76.

[42] *Ibid.*, 82.

kingdom). But the basic idea itself, as Kantorowicz has demonstrated, derives from the joining of a bishop to his diocese which
in its turn comes from Ephesians 25 where St. Paul says that
Christ and the Church form one body as do man and wife. The
marriage of the two young rulers refers simultaneously to two
ideas widely accepted in the Middle Ages; the joining of the
prince to his kingdom, and the uniting of Church and State into
one body. Both of these unions are foreshadowings of that
final unity which will come with the Second Advent of Christ.

The liturgical sequence which becomes apparent when Seringa
leaves her kingdom at the end of the Easter Octave actually has
begun earlier when Roboán left her to continue his quest. The
period of Septuagesima and Lent, and more particularly Good
Friday when Jesus was crucified, were looked upon in the Middle
Ages as commemorating the time of absence of Christ from His
Church, the Bridegroom from the Bride which was to continue
until the Parousia. [43] The great lamentation of Seringa's people
when they learn that Roboán is to leave them is comparable to

---

[43] Just as medieval man believed that all other «meanings» having to do with
Christ's mission to humanity were constantly recapitulated in history between the
moment of His Ascension and that of His Second Coming, so it was felt that the
Church annually experienced through the liturgy, the time of separation of the
earthly community from Christ, their reunion given by Jesus through His Resurrection
and finally a period which prefigured the consummate conjunction in the celestial
city. Sometimes the moment commemorating the separation of Christ from the
Christian community was taken as Good Friday; Cf. Jungmann, *The Early Liturgy,*
24. In others the entire period of Septuagesima-Lent was seen as denoting the rup-
ture. Durandus says for example while commenting on the Office for Septuagesima:
«De là vient que dans l'épître elle est averite, à l'instar de Paul, de supporter aptiement
l'absence de l'époux, et dans l'évangile, de persévérer toujours dans la semence des
bonnes oeuvres, et cette épouse qui, comme désespérée, s'était écriée d'abord...» (III,
296). John Beleth sees Septuagesima in the same way: «Septuagesima vero sonat
sexies decem, et significat tempus viduitatis Ecclesiae, ac moerorem ejus propter
absentiam Sponsi. Licet enim Christus sit nobis praesens secundum divinitatem,
juxta illud: *Vobiscum sum usque ad consummationem saeculi* (Matt. XXVIII)...
Dantur his tamen sponsae in remedium et consolationem sex opera misericordiae...
Haec sunt data sponsae, ut in eis se exerceat, utque per eorum et Decalogi observa-
tionem sibi meratur sui sponsi januam aperiri, et illius suavissimo amplexu frui»
(De Septuagesima, PL, 202, 83). One commentator. St. Martin Legionensis, in a
sermon for Easter has conceived the reunion of Christ and His bride in almost the
same manner as the author of the *Zifar.* St. Martin is discussing the events which
metaphorically take place immediately after the Resurrection: «Sic sancta virgo
Ecclesia se devovit adhaerere Christo coelesti sponso... Adipsum ergo Deum et
hominem sponsum suum cum summa devotione sancta Ecclesia de cunctis mundi
partibus concurrit, et fideliter accedit, quia se illius pretiossimo sanguine redemptam
esse cognoscit» (Sermon XXVI in Resurr. Domini, *PL,* 208, 911-912). One can
readily imagine how a creative writer might have metamorphosed the idea of the
Church hurrying from all parts of the world to her bridegroom, Christ, into the
idea of Sering journeying forth to wed Roboán.

the mourning which took place on the evening of Good Friday in the Middle Ages after the Crucifixion had been commemorated in the Mass. [44] «Dize el cuento que nunca tan grant pesar ome vio commo el que ovieron todos aquellos que y estava con la infanta; ca quando el partio de su padre e de su madre e de su hermano Garfin e de todos los otros de la su tierra, commoquier que grant pesar e grant tristeza y ovo, non pudo ser ygual desta; ca pero non se mesavan nin se rascavan, nin davan bozes, a todos semejava quel quebraran por los coraçones, dando sospiros e llorando muy fuerte y poniendo las manos sobre los oios» (429). Seringa, terribly upset herself, tells her beloved that she will wait for him for three years (429). These «tres años» doubtlessly refer to the Paschal triduum which separates the moment of Christ's death on the cross from His Resurrection, and which is the space of time when Jesus, descending into hell, is most distant from His faithful. Just as Christ rises from death after the triduum, so once the «tres años» have passed (513) Roboán sends for Seringa. He dispatches el Cavallero Amigo back to her kingdom to see if she is still waiting to marry him.

When el Cavallero Amigo arrives at her palace, the author of the *Zifar* presents us with a short vignette which is evocative of deeper meaning. «E otro dia en la mañaña fue la a ver, [Seringa] e entrando por la puerta conosçiolo, peroque non se acordava de su nonbre; e dixole: 'Cavallero commo avedes nonbre?' 'Señora', dixo el, 'Amigo'. 'Ay Cavallero Amigo!' dixo ella, 'Vos seades mucho bien venido» (510). The third chapter of the Gospel of John relates how Christ's cousin is sent before Him as a precursor to prepare for His advent into the world. The metaphor used to describe John's mission is most interesting in that it portrays him as the «friend of the bridegroom» Christ who has come to make things ready for the Son of God with His bride the Church. «He that hath the bride is the bridegroom; but the friend of the bridegroom, which standeth and heareth him, rejoiceth greatly because of the bride-

[44] Diego Marín, *La vida española* (New York, 1955), describes the attitude which still prevails in Spain on Holy Thursday and Good Friday and which must be very similar to the medieval atmosphere: «El jueves y Viernes Santo parte del tráfico se paraliza. Las mujeres se ponen mantilla negra. No se ríe a carcajadas. Reina una sensación de tristeza y de luto en la ciudad. ¡El Señor ha muerto! El viernes por la noche sale la procesión del Santo Entierro. La banda militar toca una marcha fúnebre. Todos parecen sentir la tragedia del Gólgota como si acabase de suceder allí mismo» (49).

groom's voice: this my joy therefore is fulfilled» (John 3.29). That medieval writers were aware of the dramatic possibilities inherent in this verse is borne out by Dante's use of the name Giovanna for the lady who precedes his Beatrice through the streets. «... pero che lo suo nome Giovanna e da quello Giovanni lo quale precedette la verace luce, dicendo: Ego vox clamantis in deserto: parate viam Domini.» [45] Roboán like Beatrice is *as* Christ in that he will accomplish in earthly terms what Christ will realize on the heavenly plane. Seringa is *as* the Church because she will be his bride who has waited for him so long. Thus el Cavallero Amigo acts *as* John the Baptist in going before his lord to prepare his bride for him. Giovanna preceding Beatrice in the street and el Cavallero Amigo hurrying to Pandulfa to arrange the marriage between Roboán and Seringa are «subfulfilling» the type realized in John the Baptist, the precursor of Christ who doubtless will have a true and final antitype at the end of time before Christ's Second Coming. [46]

Seringa's uncle, Ruben, played an important role in attempting to arrange the marriage between his niece and Roboán when the young knight first came to the kingdom of Pandulfa (422-423). It is to him that Seringa directs el Cavallero Amigo when he arrives to arrange the marriage. «'Traes cartas', dixo la infanta, 'para el conde Ruben mio tio?' 'Sy Señora' dixo el. 'Pues ruegovos', dixo la infanta, 'que lo fablades con el, e quel digades lo que avedes a dezir, e non le digades que fablastes comigo en esta razon'» (511).

A clue as to why the author of the *Zifar* has named the uncle Ruben may lie in Table 23 of the *Liber Figurarum* of Joachim of Flora where the Calabrian monk has arranged a series of Old Testament personages as types or figures of certain groups which have played important roles in the development of Christian history. Abraham represents the Patriarchs, Ismael the Jews, Isaac the Gentiles, Esau the Greeks, and Jacob the Latins.

---

[45] Singleton explains this use of Giovanna as a «new John» in the following manner: «It is a resemblance of analogy. This is not allegory. Where one has read *Beatrice* in the story up to now, or in the story as it continues, one may not now substitute *Christ*. Beatrice is as Christ, and because this is true, the lady who comes before her is as John the Baptist» (*An Essay on the Vita Nuova,* 22).

[46] As Jean Daniélou, *Advent,* trans. R. Sheed (London & New York, 1950) points out: «And the Fathers of the Church tell us that he (John the Baptist) will come before Him on the Last Day, that he will announce the Lord at His last Coming» (79).

Finally comes Ruben who, standing for all the twelve sons of Jacob, is the type for the «ordo clericorum». The eldest son of Jacob is used as a prefigurement for that group which in the Middle Ages was looked upon as being most closely concerned with the well-being of the mystical Church. If the author of the *Zifar* were aware of some such tradition in regard to Ruben, then it is apparent why he would have chosen this name for the character who was most concerned that Seringa (the Church) wed Roboán, an earthly type of Christ.

> «Señora, lo que vos dixe estonçe eso vos digo agora, que pues vos a casar avedes, el mejor casamiento que yo se agora e mas a vuestra onrra, este infante Roboan era». «Conde», dixo la infanta, «yo en vos pongo todo el mi fecho a la mi fazienda, que uno sodes de los de mi regno en que yo mas fio e que mas preçio; e pues lo començastes levalde adelante, ca a mi non cae fablar en tal razon commo esta». (423)

In what group does the Church have more confidence and trust than the *ordo clericorum?*

The author of the *Zifar* now concludes his eschatological imagery with the marriage of Roboán and Seringa in a monastery outside the city of Lédica on the Day of St. John the Baptist. I have pointed out that the word Lédica must be derived from Latin *lectica* which gives Spanish *lechiga*—a litter or little bed. The author seems to be giving the city a name which has the connotation of «marriage couch», and is thereby alluding to the event which will take place in it. [47] Lédica or «marriage couch» calls to mind the *lectulus* of Canticles 3.7 in which the marriage of Christ and His Church will be consummated. Throughout the Middle Ages it was of course commonplace to interpret this *lectulus Salomonis* as a figure for the celestial paradise of eternal rest and beatitude. [48] After they have been wed in the monastery,

[47] «Names and the Significance of Etymology in the *Libro del Cavallero Cifar*», 172.
[48] Examples of the *lectulus* used as a figure for the heavenly paradise are widespread, but the following give particularly good illustrations of the idea: «An non quidam paradisus lectulus Salomonis... Bene paradisus deliciarum lectulus talis» (Gillibertus de Hoilandia, *PL,* 184, 83); «Lectulus beatitudo aeterna...» (Rabanus Maurus, *PL,* 112, 983); «*Lectulus,* beatitudo aeterna, ut in Cantico: 'Lectulus Salomonis sexaginta fortes similes et operatione perfecti sunt speculantur...'» (*Ibid.,* 984); «*Lectus Salomonis* quamvis superna illius superna beatitudinis requies accipi possit, in qua sancti Dei sopitis tumultibus vitiorum, amplexu Salomonis, id ▄ viri pacifici delectantur...» (Cassiodorus, *PL,* 70, 1070). One thinks also of the «lecho» brought

Roboán and his bride go into the city where she is recognized as empress.

No more appropriate feast day could have been chosen as the date for this marriage which inaugurates a new era on this earth than the one commemorating the birth of St. John the Baptist who prepared Christ's bride the Church for Him. [49] John the Baptist is significant not only as the harbinger of Christ but also as the first sign of the new age which came upon the world with the advent of Jesus. [50] Luke 16.16 emphasizes this by pointing out that the law and the prophets ceased to be effective with John's mission because since that time «the kingdom of God is preached, and every man is pressed into it». John thus becomes the symbol of the perfection and purification of the world which had to be realized in order that the earth might be worthy of receiving the Son of God. The famous Norman Anonymous even seems to have compared an anointed king to John the Baptist in that he would have the power and opportunity to bring about perfection in his kingdom in the same way that John had achieved earthly amelioration in preparation for Christ. [51]

So the feast day of John the Baptist, on which the Church commemorates the preparation for Christ's healing ministry to man, is the optimum date for the author of the *Zifar* to choose for a marriage which will inaugurate a new era of earthly bliss. Some perfection of the earth had to be accomplished before it would be fit to receive the Son of God the first time. The author of the *Zifar* underlines his conviction that more earthly

to Oria in Berceo's *Vida de Santa Oria* (128) which also doubtless implies the eternal rest and felicity awaiting the saint.
[49] The Church still emphasizes its great debt to Christ's precursor in the Mass for June 24, as the Postcommunion prayer demonstrates: «Sumat Ecclesia tua, Deus, beati Joannis Baptistae generatione laetitiam: per quem suae regeneratione cognovit auctorem, Dominum nostrum Jesum Filium tuum...» Guéranger explains the meaning of the Secret of the Mass for St. John's Day as indicating the union of the bridegroom and the bride: «L'Epoux est en possession de l'Epouse, et c'est Jean Baptiste qui lui a préparé les voies, ainsi que le rappelle l'Antienne de la Communion. Le moment des Mystères est celui où, chaque jour, il repété: L'Epoux est celui à qui est l'Epouse; l'ami de l'Epoux qui se tient près de lui et l'entend, tressaille de joie à la voix de l'Epoux: cette joie donc, est la mienne, est complète» (III, 346).
[50] As can be seen reflected in the liturgy; cf. the first antiphon of first Vespers for the Nativity of St. John: «Ipse praebit ante illum in spiritu et virtute Eliae, parare Domino plebem perfectam.» Also a versicle for the Vigil of St. John's Day: «Ut testimonium perhiberet de lumine, et pararet Domino plebem perfectam» (*Liber antiphonarius* PL, 78, 695).
[51] See Williams, *The Norman Anonymous,* 156 and 157.

136

progress will be necessary prior to Christ's Second Coming by using St. John the Baptist's Day to initiate the joint reign of Roboán and Seringa.

Eventually a son is born to the young emperor and his wife. The child is the realization of the «new man» who will inhabit the terrestrial paradise brought into existence by the redemptive actions of his father and grandfather.

> E a cabo de un año ovieron un fijo que podriedes entender que podria nasçer de tan buen ayuntamiento commo del enperador e de la enperatris, e este fue llamado por nonbre Fijo de Bendiçion, e çiertamente bendicho fue entre todos los omes deste mundo, ca este fue onrrador de su padre e de su madre, e muy mandado a todas las cosas que ellos querian, e amador de justiçia con grant piedat, e muy granado en sus dones al que entendia que lo avia mester, de guisa que ninguno en el su señorio non era pobre nin avia ninguna mengua, sy por su grant maldat non fuese. (514-515)

That man has at long last recovered the earthly peace, harmony, and prosperity which was lost in and through Adam is demonstrated by the fact that Triguida comes to be called «Tierra de Bendiçion», an appelation taken from the name of the son (515-516). When the boy, Fijo de Bendiçion, is seven years old, Roboán and Seringa leave him in order to visit the kingdom of Seringa and to make a pilgrimage to the monastery of Santi Espiritus which Zifar had founded in the place where he first met el Ribaldo. After leaving Santi Espiritus, they go to Mentón for a reunion with Roboán's family where they spend a period of seven days. The description of this visit is one of the most movingly presented in the entire work:

> ... dize el cuento que en syete dias que moraron con el rey de Menton, non fue noche ninguna que escura paresçiese, ca tan clara era la noche commo el dia; e nunca les venia sueño a los oios, mas estavan catando los unos a los otros commo sy fuesen ymagines de piedra en un tenor, e non se moviesen. (515)

The seven days, the never-ending light and the lack of a need for sleep suggest that the author of the Zifar may have conceived this visit as a figure for that which is the most longed-for in human thought, the eventual life of the Christian in the heavenly city of God where he is to be reunited finally and forever with all family and friends (515). [52] If the author of the *Zifar* were to suggest his heavenly city in earthly terms, he would necessarily have to keep his metaphor within the bounds of an earthly meaning if he were to preserve a sense of verisimilitude. What better term could be found to figure the fellowship of the saints in heaven than a reunion with loved ones on this earth?

Immediately afterwards the typological tension of expectation relaxes. Roboán and Seringa return to Triguida where their son awaits them. The author tells us that the boy was as virtuous and worthy as his father and grandfather. To maintain his contention that all which he has been presenting is history, he tells us that a book exists in «caldeo» which recounts the adventures of Roboán's son when he grew to manhood (516). But the author's main work is done. Zifar's family is completely redeemed and there is no need to continue with other histories which might be equally valid for showing God's plan within time. The essential pattern has been demonstrated and the author can cease his work sure that he has shown the mysteries of the Christian faith in the lives of his heroes.

---

[52] Hugh of St. Victor stresses the idea that in the heavenly city no one will ever close his eyes since to do so would deprive him of the sight of God: «Durum est dicere quod sancti alia corpora tunc habebunt, ut non possint oculos claudere atque aperire cum velint; durius autem quod Deum quiquis oculos clauserunt non videbit» *(PL,* 176, 616). Berceo in *De los signos que aparescerán ante del juicio* also stresses the never-ending light enigmatically incorporating the mystic number seven, used for the number of days in the *Zifar,* as the number of suns illuminating the heavenly city: «De la primera graçia vos queremos deçir: / Aberán vida sin termino, nunca an de morir, / Demás serán tan claros, non vos cuido mentir, / Non podrían siete soles tan fuerte-mente lucir» (54).

138

BIBLIOGRAPHY

Alanus de Insulis. *Liber de Planctu Naturae*, PL, CCX (1855), cols. 431-482.
— *Liber in Distinctiones Dictionum Theologicum*, PL, CCX (1855), cols. 687-1012.
Alfonso el Sabio. *General estoria*, part. 1, ed. Antonio G. Solalinde (Madrid, 1930).
— *Opusculos legales* (2 vols. Madrid, Real Academia de la Historia, 1836).
— *Primera crónica general de España*, ed. Ramón Menéndez Pidal (2 vols., Madrid, 1955).
— *Setenario*, ed. Kenneth Vanderford (Buenos Aires, 1945).
— *Las siete partidas* (3 vols., Madrid, Real Academia de la Historia, 1807).
Alfonso, Martha. «Comparación entre el Felix de Ramón Lull y el *Caballero Cifar*, novela caballeresca a lo divino», *EL*, 12 (1968), 77-81.
Alonso, Amado. «Maestría antigua en la prosa», *Sur*, 14 (1945), 40-43.
Amador de los Ríos, José. *Historia de la villa y corte de Madrid*, i (Madrid, 1860).
Amalarius of Metz. *Liber Officialis: Opera Liturgica Omnia*, ed. Joannus Michaelus Hanssens (Vatican, 1948).
Arias y Arias, Ricardo. *El concepto del destino en la literatura medieval española* (Madrid, 1970), 222-248.
Asín Palacios, M. *La escatología musulmana en la divina comedia*, 3rd. ed. (Madrid, 1961).
Auerbach, E. «Figura», *Scenes from the Drama of European Literature* (New York, 1959), 11-76.
— *Mimesis: The Representation of Reality in Western Literature*, trans. Willard Trask (Doubleday Anchor Books, Garden City, N. Y., 1957).
Augustinus. *De Pascha: Sermo CLIX*, PL, XXXVII (1865), cols. 2058-2059.
— *Ennaratio in Psalmum 132*, PL, XXXVII (1841), cols. 1729-1736.
— *The City of God*, trans. Marcus Dods (New York, 1950).
Aulén, Gustaf. *Christus Victor*, trans. A. G. Hebert (New York and Toronto, 1931).
Ayers, Robert W. «Medieval History, Moral Purpose, and the Structure of Lydgate's *Siege of Thebes*», *PMLA*, 73 (1958), 463-474.
Baldwin, C. S. *Ancient Rhetoric and Poetic* (reprint, Gloucester, Mass., 1959).
Baillie, John. *The Belief in Progress* (London, 1950).
Beccari, Camillus. «Confessor», *CE*, 4, 215.
Bell, Dora M. *L'ideal éthique de la Royauté en France au moyen âge* (Geneva, 1962).
Berceo, Gonzalo de. *La vida de Santo Domingo de Silos*, ed. John D. Fitz-Gerald (Paris, 1904).

Bishop, Edmund. *Liturgica Historica* (Oxford, 1918).

Blake, William. *The Poetry and Prose of William Blake*, ed. David. V. Erdman (Garden City, N. Y., 1965).

Bloomfield, Morton. «Chaucer's Sense of History», *JEGP*, 51 (1952), 301-313.

— «Joachim of Flora», *Trad.*, 13 (1957), 249-311.

— «Piers Plowman as a 14th-Century Apocalypse», *Interpretations of Piers Plowman*, ed. Edward Vasta (Notre Dame, Ind., and London 1968), 339-354.

— *Piers Plowman as a 14th-Century Apocalypse* (New Brunswick, N. J. 1962).

— *The Seven Deadly Sins* (East Lansing, 1952).

Boase, T. S. R. *Boniface VIII* (London, 1933).

Bonilla y San Martín, A. *Libros de Caballerías*, ii (*NBAE* 11, Madrid, 1908).

Breviarium Gothicum, PL, LXXXVI (1891).

Brunner, F. A. «Anamnesis», *NCE*, 1, 476.

Bruyne, Edgar de. *Estudios de estética medieval*, trans. Armando Suárez (3 vols. Madrid, 1959).

Buceta, Erasmo. «Algunas notas históricas al prólogo del *Cavallero Cifar*», *RFE*, 17 (1930), 18-36.

— «Nuevas notas históricas al prólogo del *Cavallero Cifar*», *RFE*, 17 (1930), 419-422.

Burke, James F. *A Critical and Artistic Study of the Libro del Cavallero Cifar* (unpublished doctoral thesis, University of North Carolina 1966).

— «The Four 'Comings of Christ' in Gonzalo de Berceo's *Vida de Santa Oria*», *Spec* (in press).

— «The *Libro del Cavallero Zifar* and the Medieval University Sermon», *Viator*, 1 (1970), 207-221.

— «The Meaning of the *Islas Dotadas* Episode in the *Libro del Cavallero Cifar*», *HR*, 38 (1970), 56-68.

— «Names and the Significance of Etymology in the *Libro del Cavallero Cifar*», *RR*, 59 (1968), 161-173.

— «Symbolic Allegory in the Portus Salutaris Episode in the *Libro del Cavallero Cifar*», *KRQ*, 15 (1968), 68-84.

Burlin, Robert B. *The Old English Advent: A Typological Commentary* (New Haven, 1968).

Burton, Richard. *The Book of the Thousand and One Nights*, reprinted and ed. L. C. Smithers (12 vols., London, 1894).

Butcher, S. H. *Aristotle's Theory of Poetry and Fine Art*, 3rd. ed. (London, 1902).

Caplan, Harry. *Mediaeval Artes Praedicandi: A Hand-list* (Cornell Studies in Classical Philology XXIV, Ithaca, 1934).

— *Medieval Artes Praedicandi: A Supplementary Hand-list* (Cornell Studies in Classical Philology XXV, Ithaca, 1936).

Carreras y Artau, Joaquín and Tomás. *Historia de la filosofía española* (2 vols., Madrid, 1939-1943).

Cassiodorus. *Expositio in Cantica Canticorum*, PL, LXX (1865), cols. 1055-1106.

Castigos e documentos para bien vivir ordenados por el rey don Sancho, ed. Agapito Rey (Indiana University Publications: Humanities Series 24, Bloomington, Ind., 1952).

Castro, Américo. *The Structure of Spanish History*, trans. Edmund L. King (Princeton, 1954).

Castro y Calvo, José María. *El arte de gobernar en las obras de don Juan Manuel* (Barcelona, 1945).

Cavallero Cifar, Historia de, ed. Heinrich Michelant (Bibliothek des Litterarischen Vereins in Stuttgart, CXII, Tubingen, 1872).

Cavallero Zifar, El, ed. Martín de Riquer (2 vols., Barcelona, 1951).

Cavallero Zifar, El libro del, ed. Charles P. Wagner (Ann Arbor, 1929).

Charity, A. C. *Events and their Afterlife* (Cambridge, 1966).

Chiovaro, F. «Relics», *NCE*, 12, 237.

Christianus Druthmarus. *Expositio in Matthaeum Evangelistam*, PL, CVI (1864), cols. 1261-1504.

Chroust, Anton-Hermann. «The Corporate Idea and the Body Politic in the Middle Ages», *RP*, 9 (1947), 423-452.

Chydenius, Johan. *The Theory of Medieval Symbolism* (Commentationes Humanarum Litterarum XXVII, 2, Helsingfors, 1960).

— *The Typological Problem in Dante* (Commentationes Humanarum Litterarum XXV, 1, Helsingfors, 1958).

Clemente Sánchez de Vercial. *Libro de los exenplos por A. B. C.*, ed. John E. Keller (Madrid, 1961).

Cohn, Norman. *The Pursuit of the Millenium* (London, 1962).

Colish, Marcia L. *The Mirror of Language* (New Haven, 1968).

Coomaraswamy, Ananda K. *Spiritual Authority and Temporal Power* (New Haven, 1942).

Covarrubias, Sebastián de. *Tesoro de la lengua castellana o española*, ed. Martín de Riquer (Barcelona, 1943).

Curtius, Robert Ernst. *European Literature and the Latin Middle Ages*, trans. Willard R. Trask (The Bollingen Library, New York, 1963).

Daniélou, Jean. *Advent*, trans. Rosemary Sheed (London and New York, 1950).

— *Jean Baptiste* (Paris, 1964).

— *Primitive Christian Symbols*, trans. Donald Attwater (Baltimore, 1964).

Dante Alighieri, *Il Convivio*, ed. G. Busnelli and G. Vandelli (Opere di Dante, 4, Firenze, 1934).

— *La Divina Commedia*, ed. C. H. Grandgent (Boston and New York, 1909).

— *La Vita Nuova*, ed. Luigi Pietrobono, 3rd ed. (Biblioteca scolastica di classici italiani, Firenze, 1932).

Deneef, A. Leigh. «Robertson and the Critics», *CR*, 2 (1967-1968), 204-234.

Deyermond, A. D. *Epic Poetry and the Clergy: Studies on the «Mocedades de Rodrigo»* (Colección Támesis, London, 1969).

— and Walker R. M. «A Further Vernacular Source for the *Libro de buen amor*», *BHS*, 46 (1969), 193-200.

Dieter, Otto A. «*Arbor Picta*: The Medieval Tree of Preaching», *QJS*, 51 (1965), 123-144.

Dix, Gregory. *The Shape of the Liturgy* (Westminster, 1945).

Donnelly, Dorothy. *The Golden Well* (London, 1950).

Donovan, Richard B. *The Liturgical Drama in Medieval Spain* (Toronto, 1958).

Dos obras didácticas y dos leyendas, ed. Germán Knust (Sociedad de Bibliófilos Españoles, XVII, Madrid, 1878).

Durand, Guillaume. *Rationel ou manuel des divins offices,* trans. Charles Barthélemy (5 vols., Paris, 1854).

Dutton, Brian. *La «Vida de San Millán de la Cogolla», de Gonzalo de Berceo: Estudio y edición crítica* (Colección Támesis, London, 1967).

Eliade, Mircea. *The Myth of the Eternal Return,* trans. Willard R. Trask (Bollingen Series XLVI, New York, 1954).

Elliott, John R. «The Sacrifice of Isaac as Comedy and Tragedy», *SP,* 66 (1969), 36-59.

Ferrari Núñez, Angel. «La secularización de la teoría del Estado en las *Partidas»,* *AHDE,* 11 (1934), 449-456.

Fletcher, Angus. *Allegory: The Theory of a Symbolic Mode* (Ithaca and New York, 1964).

Flick, A. C. *The Decline of the Medieval Church* (reprint, New York, 1967).

Flórez, Enrique, ed. *España Sagrada,* xxxiv (Madrid, 1784).

Folz, Robert. *L'idée d'empire en occident du Ve au XIVe siècle* (Paris, 1953).

Foster, D. W. «Figural Interpretation and the *Auto de los reyes magos»,* *RR,* 58 (1967), 3-11.

Frank, Robert Worth Jr. «The Art of Reading Medieval Personification Allegory», *ELH,* 20 (1953), 236-250.

Freccero, John. «Dante's Firm Foot and the Journey Without a Guide», *HTR,* 52 (1959), 245-281.

Freytag, G. W. *Lexicon Arabico-Latinum* (Halle, 1830).

Frye, Northrop. *Fearful Symmetry: A Study of William Blake,* reprint (Princeton Paperback Edition, Princeton, 1969).

— «The Typology of *Paradisus Regained»,* *MP,* 53 (1955-1956), 227-238.

Ganshof, F. L. *Feudalism,* trans. Philip Grierson (London, Toronto, New York, 1952).

Garnerius Lingonensis Episcopus. *Sermo XVII in Die Sancto Paschae, PL,* CCV (1855), cols. 681-686.

Gelasius. *Epistola VIII, PL,* LIX (1862), cols. 41-47.

Gillebertus de Hoilandia. *Sermo XVI in Cantica Salomonis, PL,* XLXXXIV (1860), cols. 80-87.

Gilson, Etienne. «Michel Menot et la technique du sermon medieval», *RHF,* 2 (1925), 301-360. (reprinted in Gilson, *Les idées et les lettres,* 2nd ed., Paris, 1955).

— *The Philosophy of St. Bonaventure,* trans. Illtyd Trethowan and F. J. Sheed (London, 1938).

Goode, Sister Teresa C. *Gonzalo de Berceo: El Sacrificio de la Misa. A Study of its Symbolism and of its Sources* (Washington, D. C., 1933).

Grabka, Gregory. «Christian Viaticum: A Study of its Cultural Background», *Trad.,* 9 (1953), 1-43.

Green, Otis H. *Spain and the Western Tradition: The Castilian Mind in Literature from El Cid to Calderón* (4 vols. Madison, Wis., 1963).

Gregorius magnus. *Liber Antiphonarius, PL,* LXXVIII (1895), cols. 641-724.

— *Liber Sacramentorum, PL,* LXXVIII (1895), cols. 25-240.

Guéranger, Prosper. *L'Année liturgique* (15 vols. Paris, 1911).

Halverson, John. «Template Criticism: *Sir Gawain and the Green Knight*», *MP*, 67 (1969), 133-139.

Hardison, O. B. *Christian Rite and Christian Drama in the Middle Ages* (Baltimore, 1965).

Hart, Thomas H. Jr. «*El Conde Arnaldos* and the Medieval Scriptural Tradition», *MLN*, 72 (1957), 281-285.

— «Gil Vicente's *Auto de la Sibila Casandra*», *HR*, 26 (1958), 35-51.

— *La alegoría en el Libro de buen amor* (Madrid, 1959).

Hollander, Robert. *Allegory in Dante's Commedia* (Princeton, 1969).

Honig, Edwin. *Dark Conceit* (London, 1959).

Hugh of St. Victor. *De Sacramentis*, PL, CLXXVI (1880), cols. 173-618.

Isaac de Stella. *Sermon XL in Die Paschae*, PL, CLXXXXIV (1855), cols. 1824-1827.

Jacob, Alfred. «The *Razón de Amor* as Christian Symbolism», *HR*, 20 (1952), 282-301.

Javier Hernández, Francisco. «Sobre el *Cifar* y una versión latina de la *Poridat*», *Homenaje universitario a Dámaso Alonso* (Madrid, Gredos, 1970).

Joachim of Flora. *Il libro delle Figure*, ed. Leone Tondelli, Marjorie Reeves, Beatrice Hirsch-Reich (2 vols. Torino, 1953).

— *L'Evangile éternel*, trans. Emmanuel Aegerter (Paris, 1928).

Joannes Belethus. *Rationale Divinorum Officiorum*, PL, CCII (1855), cols, 14-166.

Joannes Chrysostomus. *Vidi Dominum: Homilia IV*, PG, LVI (1862), cols. 120-129.

Joannes Scotus Erigena. *Expositiones super Ierarchiam Caelestem S. Dionysii*, PL, CXXII (1865), cols. 125-266.

Johnson, E. «Easter and its Cycle», *CE*, 5, 7.

Jonas, Aurelianensis Episcopus. *Opusculum de Institutione Regia ad Pippinum Regem*, PL, CVI (1864), cols. 279-306.

Jordan, Robert M. *Chaucer and the Shape of Creation* (Cambridge, Mass. 1967).

Joyce, James. *Dubliners* (reprint, London, 1956).

Juan Manuel. *El Conde Lucanor*, ed. José Manuel Blecua (Clásicos Castalia, Madrid, 1969).

— *El libro de los estados*, ed. Pascual de Gayangos (*BAE* 51, reprint Madrid, 1952), 278-367.

— *Obras*, ed. José María Castro y Calvo and Martín de Riquer (Clásicos Hispánicos, Madrid, 1955).

Jungmann, Josef A. *The Early Liturgy*, trans. Francis A. Brunner (Notre Dame, Ind. 1959).

Kantorowicz, Ernst. *Frederick the Second*, trans. E. D. Lorimer (New York, 1957).

— «Mysteries of State: An Absolutist Concept and its Late Medieval Origins», *HTR*, 48 (1955), 65-91.

— *The King's Two Bodies* (Princeton, 1957).

Kaske, R. E. «Chaucer and Medieval Allegory», *ELH*, 30 (1963), 175-192.

— «Dante's 'DXV' and 'Veltro»', *Trad.*, 17 (1961), 185-254.

Kolve, V. *The Play Called Corpus Christi* (Stanford, Calif., 1966).

Krappe, A. H. «Le Lac enchanté dans le *Chevalier Cifar*», *BH*, 35 (1933), 107-125.

— «Le Mirage celtique et les sources du *Chevalier Cifar*», *BH*, 33 (1931), 97-103.

Ladner, Gerhart B. «Aspects of Medieval Thought on Church and State», *RP*, 9 (1947), 403-422.

— «Homo Viator: Mediaeval Ideas on Alienation and Order», *Spec.*, 42 (1967), 233-259.

Leclercq, Dom Jean. *The Love of Learning and the Desire for God*, trans. Catharine Misrahi (New York, 1961).

Lefebvre, Dom Gaspar. *St. Andrew Daily Missal* (Bruges, 1958).

Legman, G. *The Guilt of the Templars* (New York, 1966).

Levy, Bernard. «Gawain's Spiritual Journey: *Imitatio Christi* in *Sir Gawain and the Green Knight*», *Annuale Medievale*, 6 (1965), 65-106.

Lewis, Ewart. «Organic Tendencies in Medieval Political Thought», *APSR*, 32 (1938), 849-876.

Lida de Malkiel, María Rosa. *La idea de la fama en la Edad Media Castellana* (México-Buenos Aires, 1952).

— *Two Spanish Masterpieces: The Book of Good Love and the Celestina* (Illinois Studies in Language and Literature, 49, Urbana, 1961).

Locke, Frederick W. *The Quest for the Holy Grail* (Stanford, Calif., 1960).

Lomax, Derek. «The Lateran Reforms and Spanish Literature», *Iberoromania*, 1 (1969), 299-313.

Lull, Ramón. *Obres* (21 vols., Palma de Mallorca, 1906-1950).

McNeill, John T. and Gamer, Helena M. *Medieval Handbooks of Penance* (New York, 1938).

Madden, Marie R. *Political Theory and Law in Medieval Spain* (New York, 1930).

Mâle, Emile. *L'Art religieux du XIIᵉ siècle en France* (Paris, 1922).

Maimonides, Moses. *The Guide of the Perplexed*, trans. Shlomo Pines (Chicago, London, Toronto, 1963).

Marín, Diego. *La vida española*, revised ed. (New York, 1955).

Martinus Legionensis. *Sermo XXIII in Coena Domini*, PL, XXVIII (1855), cols. 865-922.

Mayer, Ernesto. *Historia de las instituciones sociales y políticas de España y Portugal* (Madrid, 1926).

Missale Mixtum secundum Regulam B. Isidori, PL, LXXXV (1862).

Mommsen, Theodore E. «St. Augustine and the Christian Idea of Progress: the Background of *The City of God*», *Medieval and Renaissance Studies*, ed. Eugene F. Rice (Ithaca, 1959), 265-98.

Montalvo, Rodríguez de. *Amadís de Gaula*, ed. Edwin B. Place, i (Madrid, 1959).

Morreale, Margherita. «Los catálogos de virtudes y vicios en las biblias romanceadas de la edad media», *NRFH*, 12 (1958), 149-159.

Murdoch, Brian. «Theological Writings and Medieval German Literature. Some bibliographical comments», *Neuphilologische Mitteilungen*, lxxi (1970), 66-82.

Navarro González, Alberto. *El mito marinero en las ínsulas* (Las Palmas, 1964).

Ong, Walter. «Wit and Mystery», *Spec*, 22 (1947), 310-341.

Osgood, Charles G. *Boccaccio on Poetry* (Princeton, 1930).

Owst, G. R. *Literature and Pulpit in Medieval England*, 2nd ed. (Oxford, 1961).

Parker, Alexander A. *The Allegorical Drama of Calderón* (London and Oxford, 1943).

Pedro de la Vega. *Flos Sanctorum* (Seville, 1568).

Pedro de Ribadeneyra. *Flos Sanctorum* (2 vols., Madrid, 1651).

Perry, T. Anthony. *Art and Meaning in Berceo's Vida de Santa Oria* (Yale Romanic Studies, Second Series 19, New Haven and London, 1968).

Petrus Lombardus. *Commentarium in Psalmos: Psalmus 132*, PL, CLXXXXI (1880), cols. 1181-1186.

Petry, Ray C. *Christian Eschatology and Social Thought* (New York and Nashville, 1956).

— *No Uncertain Sound: Sermons That Shaped the Pulpit Tradition* (Philadelphia, 1948).

Piccus, Jules. «Consejos y consejeros en el *Libro del Cavallero Cifar*», NRFH, 16 (1962), 16-30.

Pickering, F. P. *Literature and Art in the Middle Ages* (London, 1970).

Pino Saavedra, Yolando. «Exemplum de dimidio amico. De la *Disciplina clericalis* a la tradición oral chileno-argentino», *Lengua-literatura folklore: estudios dedicados a Rodolfo Oroz* (Santiago de Chile, 1967), 407-418.

Porubcan, Stefan. *Sin in the Old Testament* (Rome, 1963).

Post, Chandler Rathfon. *Mediaeval Spanish Allegory* (Harvard Studies in Comparative Literature, 4, Cambridge, Mass. 1915).

La Queste del Sainte Graal, ed. Albert Pauphilet (Les Classiques Français du Moyen Age, Paris, 1923).

Quintana, Gerónimo de. *A la muy antigua, noble y coronada villa de Madrid* (Madrid, 1629).

Rabanus Maurus. *Allegoriae in Sacram Scripturam*, PL, CXII (1878), cols. 849-1088.

— *Commentaria in Matthaeum*, PL, CVII (1864), 729-1156.

— *Homilia CLXIII, in Evangelia et Epistolas*, PL, CX (1864), cols. 135-468.

Raby, Frederick J. E. *A History of Christian Latin Poetry from the Beginnings to the Close of the Middle Ages* (Oxford, 1953).

Reeves, Marjorie. «Joachimist Influences on the Idea of a Last World Emperor» Trad., 17 (1961), 323-370.

— and Hirsch-Reich, B. «The Seven Seals in the Writings of Joachim of Fiore», RTAM, 21 (1954), 211-247.

Ricard, Robert. «Les péchés capitaux dans le *Libro de Buen Amor*», LR, 20 (1966), 5-37.

Ricardus S. Victoris. *Sermons et Opuscules Spirituels*, trans. Joseph Barthélemy De Broueur, ed. Jean Chatillon (Paris, 1951).

— *Tractatus de Gemino Paschate*, PL, CLXXXXVI (1880), cols. 1059-1074.

Robertson, D. W. *A Preface to Chaucer: Studies in Medieval Perspectives* (Princeton, 1962).

Robson, C. A. *Maurice of Sully and the Medieval Vernacular Homily* (Oxford, 1952).

Rubió y Balaguer, J. *La vida española en la época gótica* (Barcelona, 1943).

Scholberg, K. R. «La comicidad del *Caballero Zifar*», *Homenaje a Rodríguez-Moñino* (Madrid, Castalia, 1966), ii, 157-63.

— «The Structure of the *Caballero Cifar*», *MLN*, 79 (1964), 113-124.

Schramm, Percy E. *A History of the English Coronation*, trans. L. G. W. Legg (Oxford, 1937).

Scudieri Ruggieri, José. «Due note di letteratura spagnola del s. XIV», *Cultura Neolatina*, 26 (1966), 232-252.

Singleton, Charles S. *An Essay on the Vita Nuova* (Cambridge, Mass., 1949).

— «Dante's Allegory», *Spec*, 25 (1950), 78-86.

— *Dante Studies* (2 vols., Cambridge, Mass., 1954-1958).

— «In Exitu Israel de Aegypto», *Dante: A Collection of Critical Essays*, ed. John Freccero (Englewood Cliffs, N. J., 1965).

Smalley, Beryl, *The Study of the Bible in the Middle Ages*, 2nd ed. (New York, 1952).

Soons, Alan. «Towards an Interpretation of *El Caballero de Olmedo*», RF, 73 (1961), 160-168.

Spitzer, Leo. «The Prologue to the *Lais* of Marie de France and Medieval Poetics», *MP*, 41 (1943), 96-102.

Stevens, Martin. «Ritual and the Illusion of Play in the Development of the Liturgical Drama». Unpublished paper presented to the Western Michigan Conference on Medieval Studies on May 20, 1970.

Symphosius Amalarius. *Forma Institutiones Canonicorum et Sanctimoliarium*, PL, CV (1864), 815-976.

Ticknor, George. *History of Spanish Literature*, i (New York, 1849).

Tindall, William York. *A Reader's Guide to James Joyce* (New York, 1959).

Torres López, M. «La idea del imperio en el Libro de los estados de don Juan Manuel», *Cruz y Raya*, 2(1933), 63-90.

Tradiciones de Mahoma y otros sobre premios y castigos por hacer o dejar de hacer la oración. ed. Othmar Hegyi (unpublished doctoral thesis, Toronto, 1969).

Tuve, Rosemund. *Allegorical Imagery*. (Princeton, 1966).

— «Notes on the Virtues and Vices», *JWCI*, 27 (1964), 42-72.

Ullmann, Walter. *Medieval Papalism* (London, 1949).

Very, F. G. *The Spanish Corpus Christi Procession* (Valencia, 1962).

Villanueva, Jaime. *Viage literario a las iglesias de España* (22 vols., Madrid, 1850).

Von Grunebaum, Gustave. *Medieval Islam* (Chicago, 1946).

— «The Aesthetic Foundation of Arabic Literature», *CL*, 4 (1952), 323-340.

Von Richthofen, Erich. *Estudios épicos medievales*, 2nd ed. [of German original], trans. José Pérez Riesco (Madrid, 1954).

Von Simson, Otto. *The Gothic Cathedral* (New York, 1956).

Wagner, Charles Philip. «The *Caballero Zifar* and the *Moralium Dogma Philosophorum*», *RPh*, 6 (1953), 309-312.

— «The Sources of the *Caballero Cifar*», *RH*, 10 (1903), 5-104.

Walker, Roger M. «The Genesis of *El libro del Cavallero Zifar*», *MLR*, 62 (1967), 61-69.

— «The Unity of *El libro del Cavallero Zifar*», *BHS*, 42 (1965), 149-159.

— and Dutton, Brian. «*El libro del Caballero Zifar* y la lírica castellana», *Filología*, 9 (1963), 53-56.

Watts, Alan, W. *Myth and Ritual in Christianity* (London and New York, 1954).

BIBLIOGRAPHY

Wenzel, Siegfried. «'Acedia' 700-1200», *Trad.*, 22 (1966), 73-102.

Werner, Eric. *The Sacred Bridge* (New York, 1959).

White, Lynn Jr. «Christian Myth and Christian History», *JHI*, 3 (1942), 145-158.

Williams, George H. *The Norman Anonymous of 1100 A. D.* (Harvard Theological Studies, 18, Cambridge, Mass., 1951).

Williams, Margaret. *The Pearl-Poet* (New York, 1967).

Zahareas, Anthony N. *The Art of Juan Ruiz* (Madrid, 1965).

INDEX

Aaron: 78, 79n.
Adam: 31, 51, 58, 64, 66, 69, 75, 79, 81, 85, 101, 123, 128n, 137.
Advent: 14, 15, 27, 28, 119n.
Aeneas: 31.
Aenigma: 6, 7.
Agon-pathos: 59-61.
Alanus ab Insulis: 5n, 32n, 78.
Alexandrine Fathers: 21, 43.
Alfonso X: 33n, 59, 91n, 95n, 101, 118, 130.
Allegory: 8, 14, 35, 43, 45, 51, 102; conflicting meanings possible, 46; definition of, 3, 20, 23; imposition of, 47-48; of the poets, 23, 24, 24n, 30, 31, 35, 41, 42, 50; of the theologians, 3, 23n, 24, 29, 30, 31, 32, 36, 41, 49.
Amadís: 33-34, 35n, 127n.
Amalarius of Metz: 23, 129n.
Ambrose: 86.
Anagnorisis: 59-61, 62n.
Analogy-the basis of medieval thought: 20-21n.
Anamnesis-*remembranza:* 18, 18n.
Anselm: 64, 106n.
Antichrist: 113, 116, 117, 117n.
Antiphrasis: 121.
Argumentatio: 41, 43, 56.
Aristotle: 88, 90, 131.
Armenia, King of: 104.
Arming of knight: 22.
Arnald of Villanova: 117, 118.
Artes poeticae: 52.
Artes praedicandi: 39, 52, 53.
Ascension: 72.
Ash Wednesday: 65.
Asín Palacios: 76n.
Assumption: 47n, 48, 59, 61.
Auerbach, Erich: 13, 13n, 24n.
Augustine: 6, 17n, 58n, 63, 78, 86, 86n, 87, 98n, 106, 106n, 108n.
Aulén, Gustaf: 63, 64, 64n.
Ayers, Robert W: 101n.

Baillie, John: 17n.
Baldwin, C. S.: 39n.
Banner, as a symbol of virtue: 126.
Baptism of neophytes: 65; of infants, 65.

Bartholomew Iscanus: 126n.
Beard: 77-79, 83.
Beatrice: 134, 134n.
Beleth, John: 63n, 132n.
Bell, Dora M.: 87n.
Beowulf: 2n.
Bethany: 73, 74.
Bible: 5; as a source for God's plan for the world, 21; King James version, 9, 9n; literal meaning of, 43.
Bishop, Edmund: 94n.
Blake, William: 9, 9n, 10, 10n.
Blecua, José Manuel: 6n, 18n.
Bloomfield, Morton: 37n, 61n, 114n, 117, 117n, 125n, 129n.
Boat without oars: 49.
Body, as metaphor: 92-93.
Body Politic: 50, 90, 94, 98, 101, 130.
Bonaventure: 20n, 61n.
Boniface VIII: 99.
Brez, King of: 122.
Brotherhood: 106.
Buceta, Erasmo: 1n, 95n.
Buddha legend: 8.
Buen seso natural: 107, 108.
Burlin, Robert: 29n, 120n.
Burton, Richard: 76n.
Byzantine romance: 76.

Caballero de Olmedo: 47n.
Can Grande, letter to: 26, 66.
Cantar de Mio Cid: 69n.
Cantares de gesta: 33n.
Canticles 3.7: 135.
Cantigas de Santa María: 59.
Captain Ahab: 11.
Carreras y Artau, Joaquín and Tomás: 117n.
Cassiodorus: 135n.
Castigos e documentos: 92n, 125n, 129n.
Castro, Américo: 33n.
Castro y Calvo, José María: 6n.
Cavallero Amigo (el Ribaldo): 61, 127; as John, precursor of Christ, 133-134.
Cavallero Atrevido: 49, 50, 102.
Celestial Kingdom: 85, 135.
Charity, A. C.: 25n, 26, 28n, 29n, 46n, 110, 112.

149

Jiménez de Rada, Rodrigo: 33n.
Joachim of Flora: 113, 116-117, 118, 119, 128n-129n, 134.
Joannes de Rupescissa: 117n.
Job: 60.
Joel 3.18: 27.
John 13.26: 29n; 3, 133; 3.29, 134.
John and Paul, SS: 79n.
John Chrysostom: 86, 99n.
John Scotus Erigena: 23n.
John the Baptist: 134, 134n; feast of, 128, 135-137, 136n.
Jonas of Orleans: 87, 120, 120n.
Jordan, Robert: 32n.
Journey motif: 71n.
Joyce, James: 11; conception of *Ulysses* as a Mass, 12, 12n.
Juan Manuel: 8-9, 9n, 18, 22, 22n, 88n, 113, 118, 120n; ideas on empire, 87n; ideas on language, 106n; ideas on the subtle and the obscure, 7-8; ideas on verbal signs, 6; ideas on wisdom, 113; presentation of *semejanza,* 8-9, 9n; man's salvation, 52.
Judah and Benjamin, tribes: 120.
Judgment Day: 66, 85, 88.
Jung, Carl: 9n.
Jungmann, Josep A.: 16n, 132n.

Kamous: 128.
Kantorowicz, Ernst: 94, 99n, 130n, 131, 132.
Kaske, Robert: 108n, 127n.
Kernel-hull motif: 3.
King: duties of, 95-96; medieval view of his role, 87-88, 90-91, 97-98; relation with Church, 99-100.
Kings I, 12.11: 120n.
Kolve, V.: 95n.

Ladner, Gerhart: 47n, 98n.
Lady of the Lake episode: 49, 50.
Lais: 32.
Lamb, victory of: 101.
Lancelot: 40.
Langton, Stephen: 36.
Language, importance of: 106, 107.
Last Supper: 17, 17n, 18.
Laugh-emperor who never laughs motif: 123.
Leclercq, Jean: 26, 28, 44.
Lectulus Salomonis: 135, 135n.
Lédica: 128, 135.
Lefebvre, Dom Gaspar: 15.
Legman, G.: 79n.
Lent: 15, 58, 59, 63, 65, 75, 128, 132, 132n; as a period of *agon* or struggle, 63-64.
Leprosy: 101-102.
Levy, Bernard: 20n, 124n.

Lewis, Ewart: 90n.
Leyerle, John: 2n.
Liber Antiphonarius: 63n.
Liber Figurarum: 129n, 134-135.
Liber Sacramentorum: 63n.
Libro de cavalleria: 38n, 45.
Libro de buen amor: 1, 35n, 79n.
Libro del cavallero et del escudero: 6, 88n, 106n.
Libro delle Figure: 129n.
Libro de los exenplos por A.B.C.: 7.
Libro de los estados: 7, 8, 18n, 52n, 87n.
Libro de los gatos: 7.
Libro enfenido: 113n, 120n.
Lida de Malkiel, María Rosa: 2.
Light-as symbol of the celestial city: 137-138.
Lists of sins: 125n.
Literature as construction: 32n.
Literacy (*letradura*): 107.
Liturgy: 25, 58, 132n; allegorical interpretation of, 47, 127; as mystic enactment, 18, 19, 63; cosmic significance of, 16-17; evolution of, 23-24; explanation of, 14-15; significance for literature, 20-21.
Locke, F. W.: 20n.
Locus amoenus: 35.
Logos: 105, 106, 113.
Loores de Nuestra Señora: 69n, 75n.
Lope de Vega: 47n.
Losengeros: 69.
Louis VI: 127n.
Lucas de Penna: 131.
Luke 14.11: 81; 20.25, 98; 9.23, 112; 16.16, 136.
Lull, Raymundus: 38n, 45, 117, 118.
Lydgate, John: 101.
Lying: 125n.

McNeill, John T. and Gamer, Helena: 126n.
Mâle, Emile: 130n.
Marie de France: 32-33.
Marín, Diego: 133n.
Mark 4, 22-23: 105.
Marquis de Santillana: 38n.
Marriage, as a symbol of divine resolution: 110, 128-138; of king to kingdom, 91n.
Martin Legionensis, St: 132n.
Mass: 11, 17n, 18, 25, 27, 51, 59, 62, 94, 96; as drama, 25; Mozarabic, 77; use of language in, 106.
Matthew 25-parable of the good and bad servants: 40, 41, 88; 10.26, 105; 24.14, 108n.
Maundy Thursday: 65.
Maurice of Sully: 65, 72n.
Mella, port of: 59, 61.

COLECCION TAMESIS

SERIE A - MONOGRAFIAS

SERIE B - TEXTOS

CRITICAL GUIDES TO SPANISH TEXTS

(Publicadas en colaboración con Grant and Cutler Limited)

J. E. VAREY: *Pérez Galdós: Doña Perfecta.*
JENNIFER LOWE: *Cervantes: Two novelas ejemplares.*
VERITY SMITH: *Valle-Inclán: Tirano Banderas.*
D. L. SHAW: *Gallegos: Doña Bárbara.*
P. HALKHOREE: *Calderón de la Barca: El alcalde de Zalamea.*